Web Dynpro for ABAP Interview Questions, Answers, and Explanations: Unofficial WebDynpro for ABAP Certification Review

Web Dynpro for ABAP Interview Questions, Answers, and Explanations

ISBN: 978-1-60332-030-6

Edited By: Jamie Fisher

Printed in the United States of America

Please visit our website at www.sapcookbook.com

Table of Contents

Organization

Introduction

What is Web Dynpro for ABAP?

Web Dynpro is the User Interface (UI) technology for developing client-independent applications. It comes with a programming model, set of tools and a run-time. The platform independent metamodel definition enables Java and ABAP to be the run-time environment for Web Dynpro applications.

The development environment of Web Dynpro for ABAP (or, 'WD-ABAP' for short) is tightly integrated into the ABAP workbench (SE80). ABAP classes are generated automatically from the metamodel created in this design tool. Custom coding is done in ABAP for tasks such as business logic (Model) access, event handling, and dynamic screen modification. The ABAP stack of the application server (Usage type: AS-ABAP) is the runtime environment for executing the generated ABAP classes and custom coding. Based on the client from which the application is triggered, the unified rendering takes care of rendering the UI in respective technology (for example, if it is triggered from a web browser, the Web Dynpro UI metadata is converted to HTML, JavaScript and rendered using HTTP(S)).

Web Dynpro Explorer in SE80

Web Dynpro – ABAP and Java

If you are familiar with the Web Dynpro (Java) perspective in NetWeaver Developer Studio, you can appreciate the similarity between that and the above Web Dynpro Explorer (ABAP). Yes, the tools in both environments (Explorer, View editor, UI Element Outline, Property editor, etc.) are pretty comparable. Not only the tools but also the programming model, UI elements, etc. are similar in both the worlds. Due to the nature of these two worlds, there are some basic differences between these two tools, like the list of UI elements available, wizards, graphical tools and source code control & transport. I will cover the differences in detail in a future blog.

The benefits of using Web Dynpro for ABAP

Using WD-ABAP would make sense, if you are planning to develop a web application (or a non-SAPGUI application, considering) to expose the business functionality that primarily resides in the ABAP stack. Following are some of benefits of using WD-ABAP against other comparable technologies.

General Web Dynpro benefits

Since Web Dynpro is based on MVC model, your business logic is naturally separated from the presentation logic. This is a good programming practice, so that the business logic could be re-used by multiple UI applications. In the future if you decide to change the UI technology, or build another application using a different UI technology, the same business logic (Model) could be re-used.

Web Dynpro practices less-coding more-design principle. So, it is a programmer-friendly easy-to-use tool, which increases productivity.

The UI definition is stored in the form of meta-data, which is rendered dynamically at run-time by the rendering engine based on the client. This means, you don't have to learn and code using HTML / HTMLB and JavaScript (as done in technologies like BSP, JSP, etc.). I am sure the ABAPers will be glad to know that they don't have to deal with HTML & JavaScript to develop the web applications.

The flicker-free screen updates, client-side dynamics, caching, 508 accessibility support, etc. are automatically taken care of by the Web Dynpro framework.

WD-ABAP specific benefits

Since the run-time is an ABAP engine, many of the ABAP programming, DDIC and workbench elements are available inherently for WD-ABAP tools Remember that you are within the ABAP Object context, and so all relevant restrictions still apply. Don't get carried away with this power of doing SELECT-* and CALL-FUNCTION wherever you feel like. WD-ABAP is purely a UI technology and so your Model should reside separately as mentioned in the following point.
Integration of business logic (Model) in the form of Function module / BAPI / RFM, ABAP global Class, ABAP Web Service / Client proxy is seamless.
WD-ABAP applications can be deployed into SAP NW Portal as iViews and can exploit the Portal functionalities such as Portal Eventing, Object Based Navigation (OBN) etc.
Adobe Forms designed in the Form Builder (transaction: SFP), can be integrated into WD-ABAP views.

Availability

The Web Dynpro for Java has been around since SAP NetWeaver 2004. Because of this, to some extent, the term Web Dynpro itself is being used to indicate the Java flavor. As mentioned in the first paragraph, Web Dynpro for ABAP is available as part of SAP NetWeaver 2004s. This minor release of NetWeaver that is primarily meant to support mySAP Business Suite 2005 and mySAP ERP 2005, is currently under ramp-up phase. The general availability is scheduled for Q2 of 2006.
Web Dynpro for ABAP is SAP's new standard UI technology for developing user interfaces in the ABAP environment. In the long term Web Dynpro for ABAP will be the successor of the traditional screen ("Dynpro") based user interface technology which is based on the SAP GUI. Available with NetWeaver 2004s Web Dynpro for ABAP provides the same declarative UI development paradigm as Web Dynpro for Java directly out of the NetWeaver ABAP Application Server. Web Dynpro for ABAP allows the development of user interfaces directly within the ABAP Workbench (SE80) and the Web Dynpro runtime environment is a central part of the ABAP server and can be used in any SAP solution based on NetWeaver 2004s without the need of an additional server installation.

Web Dynpro for ABAP allows the development of user interfaces in a declarative way by providing a mighty framework which abstracts the rendering technology from the core UI definition tasks. The Web Dynpro developer declares the layout and behavior of the UI without caring about HTML, JavaScript, browser specifics or the HTTP protocol. Instead the focus lies on designing graphically Web Dynpro components based on the Model View Controller model, which enforces a clear separation between the UI layer and the underlying business logic.
This declarative Web Dynpro programming model enforces the developer to focus on the tasks of:

- Designing the layout of the visible views (where should the table be placed, do I need tabs, how should the button look?)
- Declaring the flow and behavior of the application (flow between views, which event is triggered by which button click...)

- Defining the data binding (which internal table is displayed in a specific table.)
- Implementing the event handlers and controller methods.

Without making any assumption about the used rendering technology, like which browser should be supported or if the Web Dynpro application will be later displayed in a web browser via HTML at all or in another kind of client with completely different rendering capabilities.

The Web Dynpro Frameworks provide all important UI features directly out of the box:

- All elements (tables, buttons, trees, dropdown list boxes...) necessary for state of the art user interfaces are provided by the Web Dynpro Framework in the form of predefined UI element libraries.
- Complex features and behavior of UI elements.
- Internationalization of the UI. All visible strings in a Web Dynpro ABAP UI are handled by the translation system and are translated in the same translation environment like other ABAP language dependent resources. All texts are displayed automatically at runtime, dependent of the user's credentials
- Accessibility features are directly built into the framework and UI elements.
- A unified rendering engine generates at runtime the data that is sent to the specific client application, which is not limited to browsers but includes the NetWeaver Business Client.

All this is available in the established environment of the ABAP application server and well known capabilities like the transportation and change management system, security environment, test and performance analysis tools or remote debugging can be used like in common ABAP development.

Designing the Layout

Question 1: Dropdown by Index

I have created a 'Drop Down' by index in a Webdynpro program. How can I populate it?

A: You can try creating a context node which contains the elements for the dropdown. One attribute of this structure is that it should contain the text you want to display in the drop down. Then, bind the text property of the dropdown to this attribute.

For example:

```
node (cardinality 0..n or 1..n)
--- attribute customer name
--- attribute customer number
```

Bind the attribute customer name to the text's attribute of dropdown by index, and then all names will be displayed. Fill this node in supply method for example.

Afterwards, you can get the selected element via the lead selection.

If you set initialize lead selection, the first element of the node will be pre-selected in the drop down.

You can also consider a simple scenario where you want to display 'yes' and 'no' in your drop down. Bind the 'TEXTS' property of your drop down with a node attribute. You can give the cardinality of the node as "0..n" and selection as "0..1". For this example, consider the node name as 'dropdown'.

```
DATA lo_nd_dropdown TYPE REF TO if_wd_context_node.
data: Stru_dropdown type If_Main=>Elements_dispose,
wa_stru_dropdown TYPE wd_this->element_dispose.
* navigate from <CONTEXT> to <DISPOSE> via lead
selection
lo_nd_dropdown = wd_context->get_child_node( name =
wd_this->wdctx_dropdown ).

wa_stru_dropdown-DEACTIVATE_VAL = 'Yes'.
INSERT wa_stru_dropdown INTO TABLE Stru_dropdown.
wa_stru_dropdown-DEACTIVATE_VAL = 'No'.
INSERT wa_stru_dropdown INTO TABLE Stru_dropdown.
```

```
lo_nd_dropdown->bind_elements( Stru_dropdown ).
```

This should fill up your pop up by values 'yes' and 'no'. Basically, you are just binding a table containing the desired values with the node.

Also, check the webdynpro component "WDR_TEST_EVENTS", which is an example when to use various UI elements. There is a view for drop down by index also, that will be of help to you.

The example code is just an EXAMPLE create with the wizard, you have to build your own node in your context for the drop down elements.

Question 2: Table pop-in

I have a table pop-in within a standard SAP structure. For this node entry, I made two sub-nodes, one with the sub-table content and one with the "table_popin" id. When I click the table, I always get some sort of dump.

What is the correct way to set the nodes to make this work?

A: Create one sub-node which contains the string of the table pop-in name. The table pop-in property of the table is bound to this node.

Open the pop-in with a "LinkToAction" where you receive the actual element and the name is set in the sub-node of this element. The table which is shown inside the pop-in is also bound to a sub-node.

The sub-node with the pop-in name has a cardinality of 1:1 (init lead select is set too). The items of the pop-in table is '0:n' and the table itself is also '0:n'.

Question 3: View designer layout tab display problem

I am trying to create a web dynpro component. I am getting a 'page not found error' in the layout tab of the view. I tried to follow all the steps given by activating all the ICF services needed.

What should I do next?

I wanted to know further on the IE settings. What should I know on this? Usually in the settings, the values have to be set in SAP or ICF nodes in able to be activated.

A: You can try to navigate to the following directory:

C:\WINDOWS\system32\drivers\etc;

after following path, you will find a Hosts File then edit it. Just give your applications server for ex. 10.112.49.45 local host. After adding the string and it works, save.

Another analysis for your situation is that you were not able to link to WAS. You will have to change your internet explorer settings. Contact your administrator or try to change the settings manually.

Just for information, for Web dynpro ABAP, SAP ECC 6.0 onwards is required and WAS 7.0 is a must. Only then you will be able to see the layout preview and can run the application in the internet explorer.

In the previous preliminary versions, there were several other values in addition to delta (default value of server-side delta rendering) and double Buffer. An example for this is raw (for test purposes) and embedded (for portal integration). Before server-side rendering was introduced as standard, there was a client-side framework which was dropped in favor of server-side rendering.

Also, make sure all the configuration settings are done.

For the settings, you can try this:

1. Activate "WDT_QUIZ" in SICF under **default_host->bc->webdynpro->sap->** right click **wdt_quiz** and select 'activate service'.

2. Go to SE80 and take a look at "WDT_QUIZ" . Expand Web Dynpro Applications and double click 'wdt_quiz'. On the right hand side on the bottom, you should see an entry for URL something like

http://yourcompanyname:8090/sap/bc/webdynpro/sap/wdt_quiz.

It seems like this URL cannot be accessed most likely because **yourcompanyname** is not a FQDN of the application server (fully qualified domain name - perhaps it should be **http://www.yourcompanyname.com:** or something like that).

What you can do is: (first, check if my assumption is correct)

1. Go to Start->run->cmd on your PC and ping your FQDN like - ping www.yourcompanyname.com and then get the IP address.

2. Go to the host file on your PC **c:\WINDOWS\system32\drivers\etc\hosts** and all the way on the bottom, enter the following, separated by tabs: The IP address the FQDN and the domain name that you saw under URL in "wdt_quiz". So the entry will look something like this:

333.4.0.1. www.yourcompanyname.com yourcompanyname

Save it and try to go back to SE80. If that worked, contact your system admin and have him/her configure correct FQDN. It is done in RZ11 for 'icm/host_name_full' (I believe).

Question 4: Layout – Grid or Matrix

How can I place two tables and in between these two tables, 2 buttons that are placed one on top of the other?

In principle, I have three columns. In the second column, there should be 2 buttons vertically aligned.

I tried with grid layout (column count 3) but the buttons are not one on top of the other.

Which layout do I have to use and which properties do I have to set?

A: You should use the transparent container element. In there, place the two buttons on top of each other and set the container in between the tables. In your container, you can e.g. use matrix layout and set the layout type for each button to matrix head data or a grid layout with only one column.

Another suggestion is in the middle column of the grid, embed a transparent container. Set the layout of this container to grid layout (1 Column) and then embed the buttons here.

Question 5: Changing the text of the button dynamically

I have a requirement of changing the text of the button dynamically when I click it.

In the event handler of that button, I want to change the text for that button and change its functionality as well.

How can I do that?

How can I display pop-ups?

I want an input field and an 'ok' button in the popup.

When I say 'ok' in the popup, I should be able to read the value entered by the user.

How can I accomplish these tasks?

A: You can use the Web dynpro code wizard (Ctrl + F7) to create a popup window. But before using the code wizard, create a window and embed whatever views you want to show in a popup window.

However, if you are want to just show a message in a popup, you can use the following code to do it:

```
  DATA: l_cmp_api           TYPE REF TO
if_wd_component,
        l_window_manager    TYPE REF TO
if_wd_window_manager,
        l_popup             TYPE REF TO if_wd_window,
        l_text              TYPE string_table,
        l_api               TYPE REF TO
if_wd_view_controller.
  DATA message type string.

  l_cmp_api          = wd_comp_controller->wd_get_api(
).
  l_window_manager = l_cmp_api->get_window_manager(
).

  Message = 'Your message here.!'.
  append message to l_text.
```

```
  l_popup = l_window_manager-
>create_popup_to_confirm(
                TEXT          = l_text
                button_kind   =
if_wd_window=>co_buttons_ok
                message_type  =
if_wd_window=>co_msg_type_information
                window_title  = 'Information'
                window_position =
if_wd_window=>co_center ).

  l_popup->open( ).
```

Another way for creating pop-ups is to get a reference to your window manager by calling the following:

```
lr_comp_api = wd_comp_controller->wd_get_api( ).
window_manager = lr_comp_api->get_window_manager( ).
```

Now, call method "create_popup_to_confirm" which will return you a window object. Call method "window->open" to open the popup.

You can try the following to change the button text:

In the modify view method, get the reference of your button by passing the ID of the UI element.

```
lr_button type ref to cl_wd_button.
lr_button ?= view->get_element( 'ID' ).
```

Now, you can do a "lr_button->set_text", "bind_action", etc.

The simplest way to change the text of the button dynamically is to bind the text property to a context attribute. Then, simply change the context attribute to the new text and automatically the button text will change to the new value.

As for the functionality, you can bind only one event handler to a button. So, inside the event handler, have the logic based on the button text.

For example:

```
case button_text.
 when 'ONE'.
   "do processing required when button text is ONE.
 when 'TWO'.
   "do processing required when button text is TWO.
endcase.
```

The "button_text" here refers to the actual text that is set for the button.

What you need to do is as follows:

1. Read the context attribute that you have bound to the button's text property into a variable called "button_text".

2. Use this variable for the **case** statement.

You can put this code in the controller and call it in the view.

```
Data:l_cmp_api type ref to if_wd_component,
l_window_manager type ref to if_wd_window_manager,
l_comp_info type ref to IF_WD_RR_COMPONENT,
l_final_window type ref to IF_WD_WINDOW.

l_cmp_api = wd_this->wd_get_api( ).

CALL METHOD L_CMP_API->GET_COMPONENT_INFO
RECEIVING
COMPONENT_INFO = l_comp_info
.

* CALL METHOD L_COMP_INFO->GET_WINDOW
* EXPORTING
* WINDOW_NAME = 'W_POPUP'
* RECEIVING
* RESULT = l_com_window
* .
l_window_manager = l_cmp_api->get_window_manager( ).

CALL METHOD L_WINDOW_MANAGER->CREATE_WINDOW
EXPORTING
* MODAL = ABAP_TRUE
WINDOW_NAME = 'W_POPUP'
* TITLE =
* CLOSE_BUTTON = ABAP_TRUE
* BUTTON_KIND =
* MESSAGE_TYPE = IF_WD_WINDOW=>CO_MSG_TYPE_NONE
* CLOSE_IN_ANY_CASE = ABAP_TRUE
```

```
* MESSAGE_DISPLAY_MODE =
* DEFAULT_BUTTON =
RECEIVING
WINDOW = l_final_window
.


wd_this->LO_POPUP = L_FINAL_WINDOW.


CALL METHOD L_FINAL_WINDOW->OPEN
.
```

The window name provided is the name of the window that you created where you embedded the views for the pop up.

Save the instance in the controller to close the window in the future.

These are other steps to achieve your functionality:

1. Create a new view (say, view_input) and place your input field there. In fact, you can design this view just like any other view, with any number of controls. Do not place the 'OK' button inside this view. The 'OK' button will be present automatically when you create the popup window.

2. Map the relevant context attributes to this view and to the 'inputfield' in the view. Create a new window (say, win_pop) and embed the above view into it.

3. Now, in your main view, the place where you want to call the popup window, use the following code:

```
  data lo_window_manager type ref to
if_wd_window_manager.
  data lo_api_component  type ref to if_wd_component.
  data lo_window         type ref to if_wd_window.

  lo_api_component  = wd_comp_controller->wd_get_api(
).
  lo_window_manager = lo_api_component-
>get_window_manager( ).
  lo_window         = lo_window_manager-
>create_window(
                     window_name          =
'WIN_POP'
*                    title                =
```

```
*                          close_in_any_case      =
abap_true
                           message_display_mode   =
if_wd_window=>co_msg_display_mode_selected
*                          close_button           =
abap_true
                           button_kind            =
if_wd_window=>co_buttons_ok
                           message_type           =
if_wd_window=>co_msg_type_none
                           default_button         =
if_wd_window=>co_button_ok
                           ).
  lo_window->subscribe_to_button_event(
                 button              =
if_wd_window=>co_button_ok
                 action_name         = 'ON_OK_POPUP'
                 action_view         = wd_this-
>wd_get_api( )
                 is_default_button = abap_true ).

  lo_window->open( ).
```

4. In the above, 'On_OK_POPUP' is an action that is called when the user clicks on the 'OK' button in the popup window. For this, you have to create an action with this name in the 'Main view'. Whatever you want to do after the popup window is closed, you have to put the code inside this method. To read the value entered in the popup window, just read the context attribute to which it was bound.

In the attribute section of the view, you have to make the following declaration:

```
Attribute: wd_this
Ref to: check this checkbox
associated type: IF_VIEW_NAME
```

Replace view_name with your view name. I think it should be IF_ACTION_VIEW in your case.
"Wd_this" will be automatically created; you don't have to manually create it. You should not create it as a parameter. It is an attribute that you will find in the attributes section of your view.

Please check where you are writing the code in the controller or something. Also, write the code in the view. Please verify that you are writing the code inside a method/action in your **view** and not anywhere else.

Question 6: Space between two fields

In dynpro, how can we get the space between two elements and the next line, and align the fields in the center?

Can we use HTML or like javascript in dynpro?

If a user press login button, then after checking from the database whether the username password is correct in the main view call, and if the user presses the new user button, the new user view is called.

How can I achieve this functionality?

A: For spacing, you can specify the "paddingleft", "paddingright", "paddingtop", and "paddingbottom" properties of the element. This is available only if you use the grid layout.

You can define the spacing between elements in your layout. For example, if you specify the layout of your container (group/tray etc) as "Grid Layout", in the properties, you can specify the cell padding.

Space can be arranged only with the correct layout, if you choose a grid layout there will be a space.

To achieve this, you need to have three views:

```
view1 = login page
view2 = Home page
view3 = new user page
```

In the view1, you need to create two outbound plugs, one for view2 and other for view3.

In view2 and view3, you need to create inbound plugs from view1.

Go to the window and embed the views, then create the navigation links between the different plugs.

Now in your login button action, write the following code:

```
if user exists in database.
Fire out bound plug for view2 - homepage
else.
Fire outbound plug for view3 - New user page
endif.
```

For your second requirement, create a context node "login" with username and password fields. Bind the attributes to your input fields. On click of the button, in the event handler, read the context attributes. Pass them to your API, say "verify_details" (username, password). Depending on the result, you either display an error message or fire a navigation plug.

You need to define an outbound plug between your login view and user view. You can use the wizard to fire the outbound plug.

To display a message, you need to use the interface "if_wd_message_manager".

For navigating to two different views, you can create two outbound plugs from your current view (one plug each to the two target views). Then, depending on the validation, you can fire the required outbound plug.

To fire the outbound plug, you can use the code wizard. Firing the outbound plug will automatically allow you to navigate to the next view.

Question 7: Define the class in the attribute of the view

The new problem is I defined the global class and all my methods for checking the data base are in the global class.

If I use the method of class in the 'onclick' of button action, the following works:

```
data : web_class type ref to zcl_web_class.
create object web_class
call web_class-> check_login.
```

But if I want to define the instance of my class 'zcl_web_class' in the whole view, it didn't work. I tried to define that class in the attribute of the view.

Is there a fix for this?

A: You can add an attribute of the type "zcl_web_class" in your view attribute. But it depends where you are going to create an instance and save it to that attribute. Otherwise, if you populate the attribute with an instance value, it will not work. I will suggest that in your "domodifyview", do the following method:

```
if first_time = abap_true
```

(create an instance of web class and save the instance in the view attribute)

```
endif.
```

Another place to put your 'create object..' statement would be in the 'wdoninit' method. This method call happens only when the view is loaded for the first time.

Also, while creating the object in the attributes section, put a tick mark on the 'ref to' checkbox.

You can also create an instance in the 'doinit' and save it as a class attribute of your view. Or use static method to make the whole thing simpler.

Question 8: Call method of class

As suggested, I defined the object in the 'attribute tab' of the view with 'ref to' mark as checked:

```
web_class type ref to ZCL_WEB_CLASS
```

After that, I created the instance in the 'wdoinit' and even tried with modify as:

```
create object web_class
```

After defining all these, when I call my method of class in the "ONACTIONON_LOGIN_1" action, it stated "error web class not define".

```
CALL METHOD web_class->login
```

What's wrong now?

A: First suggestion is to access the instance as "wd_this->web_class".

Another suggestion is the call should be like the following:

```
wd_this->Web_class->login.
```

It should not be directly the attribute.

Lastly, you have to refer it as "wd_this->web_class". The correct call would be:

```
call method wd_this->web_class->login.
```

Also, ensure that you have the create object statement only in the 'wdoninit' method.

Question 9: Change Series Color in Business Graphic control

I changed the color of series in chart designer, but in runtime the color didn't change.

I changed the number of value axis main tick, but in runtime it didn't change.

How can I fix this?

A: The series settings can only be used if you use its ID in the data as well. Check 'customizingID' that tells the chart engine which data series uses which series customizing. Concerning the last issue, I recommend you to check if the latest IGS patch is installed.

Question 10: Text disappears when the pop-up is opened

The button text disappears when I open the pop-up. I'm using the guided activity. In the step-3, I displayed the list of documents. When the user clicks on the document, the document details have to be displayed in the pop-up. When I open the pop-up, the button text disappears in the View 'V_STEP3'.

What could be the reason for this?

A: Find the pop-up state and check where you are setting the text dynamically, or otherwise just add the state and put some text in it.

You can also go to the relevant method and check the case condition. You might have missed the state of popup to include, when text for the button is generated.

Question 11: Error when registering events to pop-up button

I encountered an error when trying to register events to popup button: What step did I miss for the correct setup? This is the code that caused the exception:

A: If you have written the code "e_popup->open( )" in the middle of your code segment; it needs to be sent to the very end.

First, create the window which you have done, then set the properties like default button, button kind, and size. If you want to handle the event by the buttons in the window, subscribe it then open the window. So, it's the last step which you have done in the middle and causes the problem.

The "set_button_kind" and "set_default_button" are not required, and "window->open( )" should be called after 'subscribe to button' event. That should be at the end. Make sure that you mention the action name and not the method name.

Question 12: Set rows in ALV to editable or non-editable

I'm creating an ALV table where the user can enter a data and then this will be uploaded into the system. Now, upon validation some records might fail and would need some changes, and some records that had no problems would be successfully posted.

When the program returns to the user, I want the successful one's to be grayed out and not editable. I'm not sure on how I could access the rows of the table. I tried few classes and all I could manage was to change the table setting and configurations.

A: Have an input field as cell editor for your editable column. Bind the 'read_only' property of your input field to that context attribute 'read_only'. Depending on the validation, just set this field to read only or editable and do a 'bind_elements' to your node.

Question 13: Align fields or label in Web Dynpro

How can I align label, fields, or other object in a view of Webdynpro?

I've created a view and tried different layouts, but if I insert labels and inputfields, I can't align them.

If I have a grid layout and two fields with two label (label1-text: Name: label2-text=Your father's name:) with different size, I can't align the input.

If I have 8 or 9 label and input fields, and I want to show in one row 2 label and 2 input fields, in another row 3 label and 3 input field, in the other row 1 label and 1 input field. The labels have different sizes.

How can I align the inputfields?

A: You have the various layouts to do the alignment. If you choose a grid layout, you can specify how many fields or UI elements you want to display in a single row by giving the col count. You can adjust the cell padding to determine the spacing between elements.

In a matrix layout, for every new line of elements, give the data type as Matrix head data. All other elements will be Matrix data. A row layout also works similarly.

Try creating views with different layouts.

You cannot align them by drag and drop or something. Based on the properties of your layout, they will get aligned. So it is a good idea to decide on your layout and then start designing the view.

If your container width is 100% and you only have like 2 fields (two columns) in combination with the parameter stretched horizontally, you have to spread them around. If you don't spread, the columns will be aligned on the left side of your screen with normal dimensions if you leave the container width blank.

You can custom design by setting the number of pixels in the "width" property to change its display on the screen. Eg: 1200px will make the UI element 1200px long. You will have to do trial and error to see what works best for your screen.

If you want the fields to appear as you have specified, i.e label: name, label2: name2, set the 'colcount' property of your grid to 4.

One way to do this would be as follows:

Set the 'rootuielement' container's layout as flow layout. The elements will come one below the other.

For each of the row of input that you want, have a transparent container. So if you want 3 rows, essentially your root should have 3 transparent containers. Inside each transparent container, have your labels and input fields.

In the first container, set the layout as grid will col count = 4. Keep the width of the container as 100% so that it spans the whole screen. In the second container, keep the col count as 6. In the 3rd one, col count = 2. If all the widths are 100%, the input field sizes would get automatically adjusted.

You can also go for a Matrix layout and whenever you want to display a UI element, say a label in the next row, make its layout data as "MATRIXHEADDATA" instead of "MATRIXDATA".

Eg: you want to show 2 input fields with label in the first row, and 3 input fields and their labels in the next row.

All you need to do is to place them in a transparent container or a group. Make the layout property of it as "MATRIXLAYOUT".

Then, make the 1st label as "MATRIXHEADDATA" leave 1st inputfield, 2nd label 2nd inputfield as "MATRIXDATA".

Again, make 3rd label as "MATRIXHEADDATA", and the remaining labels and inputfield of that line as "MATRIXDATA".

Question 14: Preventing a pop-up from closing

I've written a pop-up with an input box. I'd like to prevent the pop-up from closing if the user hasn't entered anything in the input box.

I open the pop-up from one view via the following code:

```
DATA: l_cmp_api TYPE REF TO if_wd_component,
l_window_manager TYPE REF TO if_wd_window_manager.

l_cmp_api = wd_comp_controller->wd_get_api( ).
l_window_manager = l_cmp_api->get_window_manager( ).
IF wd_this->m_add_popup IS INITIAL.
wd_this->m_add_popup = l_window_manager-
>create_window(
window_name = 'ADDWINDOW'
button_kind = if_wd_window=>co_buttons_okcancel
message_type = if_wd_window=>co_msg_type_information
).
ENDIF.

lo_api = wd_this->wd_get_api( ).
wd_this->m_add_popup->subscribe_to_button_event(
button = if_wd_window=>co_button_ok
action_name = 'OK'
action_view = lo_api
is_default_button = abap_true ).

wd_this->m_add_popup->open( ).
```

I tried putting validation in the "WDDOBEFOREACTION" method in the "ADDVIEW".

E.g.

```
l_current_controller ?= wd_this->wd_get_api( ).

CALL METHOD l_current_controller->get_message_manager
RECEIVING
message_manager = l_message_manager.
.

CALL METHOD l_message_manager-
>report_fatal_error_message
EXPORTING
message_text = 'Error - Please enter a quantity and
date'.
```

```
exit.
```

If I write out a message via the message manager, it appears in the calling view and not in the pop-up. Regardless of what I do, the pop-up always seems to close.

What can be the remedy for this?

A: You have to set the following where you open the pop-up window:

```
window  type ref to if_wd_window.
wd_this->window->set_close_in_any_case( abap_false ).
```

Now, the pop-up only closes when you call the close method of "IF_WD_WINDOW". So you can make your validation and close the pop-up window only when the entries are ok.

Question 15: Registering custom button events to pop-up

I'm currently working with pop-ups in Web dynpro ABAP. When creating and opening a pop-up, we can register an action in the main window. When a certain button in the pop-up was clicked, the action in the main window can be performed. But it looks I can only register the action for pre-defined button like 'OK', 'Yes', 'NO', etc, or register on close action. When I tried to create my own button from web dynpro, I can't find out how to register an action in the main window which corresponds to this click button.

How can I register a custom button event to pop-up? If I have my own button which is a standard abap web dynpro button, how can I register a main window action for this button?

This button is not the type window pop-up button. I can't find the function to register an event for it. I can only trigger "window->close" when the button is clicked, but the action in the main window can not be performed.

Is it also possible to fire the action in the main window's view via the button in the pop-up view?

A: Get a reference to your window manager, and create a window object as a pop-up window. For this, use the method "window_manager->create_popup_to_confirm" that would return a reference to "if_wd_window".

You then need to call the method 'window->subscribe' to button event for each button you wish to have. If you have a yes/no/cancel, subscribe to button event thrice, passing the action as "yes", "no", "cancel" etc. These actions need to be defined separately in the "Actions" tab of your view. The event handlers will be created automatically. After defining the actions, call the method "window->open" to display your pop-up window.

I think only the pre-defined set of button works. Below is the list:

```
CO_BUTTONS_ABORTRETRYIGNORE
CO_BUTTONS_OK
```

```
CO_BUTTONS_CLOSE
CO_BUTTONS_OKCANCEL
CO_BUTTONS_YESNO
CO_BUTTONS_YESNOCANCEL
CO_BUTTON_NONE
CO_BUTTON_ABORT
CO_BUTTON_RETRY
CO_BUTTON_IGNORE
```

Also, in the "IF_WD_WINDOW->SUBSCRIBE_TO_BUTTON_EVENT" method, the button should be the type "WDR_POPUP_BUTTON" and it has a value list now. This means you cannot use your own value for the time being. Maybe they will come up with an enhancement in the future. So till that time, I don't think you will be able to use your own buttons.

If you are talking about registering an action for a normal button, go to the properties tab of your button element. You would see a field "On Action". You can create your own event there. This will be called when you click the button, and the event handler "onaction<event name> method" will be generated. Do your processing there.

Meanwhile, if the pop-up you mean is just a modal dialog like a prompt for save or something, then it will be in the same window as your main view. You will create a window object and call it in the modal format. It will not be a new view.

But I think you are talking about displaying a view as a pop-up. In that case, I do not think you can trigger an event in your main view from the pop-up view.

Another way is to trigger an action in the main view through a pop-up action. The thing is that, your pop action will be part of your main view. So in your pop-up action, you could call your main view method or event.

like call method mainviewmethod ( ).

Question 16: Drop down visibility or invisibility

I have one view and in this view, it has some step from the drop down box. Now, on the click of this value selected in the drop down, I want to set the visibility or invisibility of some transparent container to 'true' or 'false'.

Currently, this job was done in 'WDDO_INIT' of View2. In that, I have filled the context node of the visibility flag. But the problem occurred when I go back to the previous view and changed the value in the drop box. It showed me the transparent container visible which was there from the previous selected drop down.

What method is called every time the view is loaded?

A: The modify view method is called for every action on your view. For this case, I think you can write the code in the 'onSelect' event of the drop down and setting the flag to 'true' or 'false'. You also need a check in the inbound plug handler into your view.

Another suggestion is you have to call the method in the 'WDDOMODIFY', and not in init.

"wddo_init" is called only on the first time for each screen.

Also make sure that when you are going back to the drop down, you have restored the original visibility of the transparent container. This will ensure that your previously selected visibility options do not appear when you do a selection from the drop down next time.

Question 17: Splash screen

When I start Web dynpro application in 'IVIEW', it splashes one 'NETWEAVER Screen'.

Can I ignore that?

A: On Web Dynpro application (SE80), you can find the "WDDISPLAYSPLASHSCREEN" parameter.

Have a look at the OSS note 891525.

Question 18: Creating the drop down list in Web Dynpro

How can I create the drop down list in web dynpro application?

A: Take a look at the example component "WDR_TEST_EVENTS" and the two views DROPDOWNBYIDX" and "DROPDOWNBYKEY".

Examples of the Display

Question 19: Reference on interface controller

My "COMPONENTCONTROLLER" has an interface method which needs to be called outside the web dynpro component. To be more specific, this method needs to be called in an ABAP OO class, not in a using component.

Therefore, I want to transfer a reference on the interface controller (IWCI_<component>) to the ABAP OO class. How can I create a reference on the interface controller (in the component of the interface controller)?

A: You mean you want to call a WD components method outside WD component (within the lifetime of the component) in a class.

One of the possibilities is to use the 'Assistance class' for the Web Dynpro Component. You should have an attribute in the assistance class. In the assistance class, we can have attributes referencing to "IF_WD_CONTEXT_NODE", message manager. We can access the context and we can process the context from the assistance class.

You could also just pass "wd_this" as reference, if you are in the component controller.

Lastly, the below code snippet may help you to acess the interface method of the web dynpro component in an ABAP class:

```
lo_interface_controller TYPE REF TO
abap_interface_controller.
```

(to get ABAP interface name, go to web dynpro component interface -> go to interface controller -> properties-> ABAP Class name, is the interface which needs to be used in the programming)

```
lo_interface_controller ?= wd_this.
```

(reference to Component controller of your webdynpro

component in which above interface method is being used)
lo_interface_controller->interface_method( ).

Now, you can use this interface controller's reference to access
the method of that interface.

Question 20: WDA stylesheet via sap-cssurl parameter

I'm customizing my web dynpro abap application with my CSS stylesheet. "WDA - Custom themes for Web Dynpro ABAP applications without SAP Enterprise Portal integration" which supplies precious informations. But when I test my stylesheet, it doesn't work.

What can be the solution for this?

A: Try to save theme not to /SAP/PUBLIC/BC/UR/customerthemes/bcp but for example /SAP/PUBLIC/BC/customerthemes/bcp.

You can download in your desktop the theme 'sap_tradeshow' in an empty folder. Modify what you need. For example, to change CSS, select folder and change the file "ur_nn6.css (for filefox)", "ur_ie6.css (for internet explorer version 6)".
At the end, use the same report "BSP_UPDATE_MIMEREPOS" to upload your new customer theme (follow the path '/SAP/PUBLIC/BC/UR/customerthemes/<your theme>').
Remember to go in transaction SICF, under 'public/bc' and create the sub-element, 'customerthemes'. It must heave in the handler list the class "CL_HTTP_EXT_WEBDAV_PUBLIC".

Question 21: Web Dynpro View Layout Preview Problem

I'm trying to develop a WDA application. Our servers are upgraded recently from 4.6C to ECC 6.0.

When I incorporate view and go to layout tab while developing, the system gives me a proxy error, "page can't be displayed".

What is HTTPPURLOC table? How can I configure it?

A: This is a Basis configuration problem with the underlying installation. You should not be afraid to call upon other resourcse on a project to complete their component of the work when you run into an unknown problem.

Question 22: Standard text in Adobe form

I want to pass 'Standard Text' to Adobe form which I created in SO10. In 'smartform' and 'SAPScript', we can go to editor and include the standard text in it. I want to do it in Adobe form.

How can I do this?

A: Create a Text Module

Question 23: To populate blank value in 'dropdownbykey'

I am using 'dropdownbykey' UI element. I defined a method to populate the value.
But once I selected a value from the drop down, I was not able to select the blank value again.

Is there any method to populate the 'get the blank value in the drop down?

Can we do something related with the UI element properties even if not programatically?

A: Just add a key value pair with an empty value where you populate the values.

'DropDownByKey' requires some lines of code. There is one exception which is using a 'datatype' (datalement) attached to a domain with fixed values. The fixed values, defined in the dictionary, will populate the drop down.

'DropDownByIndex' uses a different approach, it dedicated a node in the Context which makes it easy to populate via 'Supply Function'.

Without programatically, we can't achieve this functionality. As was suggested, we need to insert a blank key, and a value in the table which we bind to the node's attribute.

Question 24: Dynamic creation of checkbox

I want to dynamically create a checkbox in the layout. Is there a sample coding on how to create the same?

A: You can try the following code:

```
lo_container ?= m_view->get_element( 'name of layout
container' ).

lo_checkbox = cl_wd_checkbox=>new_checkbox(
bind_checked = attribute_path
id = attr_ui_element_id
view = m_view ).

cl_wd_'layout type' =>new_'layout type'_data( element
= lo_chackbox ).

lo_container->add_child( lo_checkbox ).

with layout type eg grid_layout
```

The "attribute_path" is something like 'NODE1.SUBNODE1.ATTRIBUTENAME', depending on the nodes in your context - what you get in the check box when you declare your checkbox on 'designtime'.

'attr_ui_element_id' is your id on your view. This is what you put in the id field in the layout pane, naming conventions point at CKB_'name of checkbox' as id.

'm_view' is the instance of the view. In 'wddomodifyview', it's an importing parameter, and you should bind it to the 'attribute m_view' in the view attributes.

Put this in 'wddomodifyview':

```
if first_time is not initial.
wd_this->m_view = view.
endif.
```

In the attributes pane: 'm_view type' ref 'to if_wd_view'.

Question 25: Drop down box in Web Dynpro

My requirement is to create the drop down list. When I select the value from the list, I have to display the table's value according to that selected value.

For this, I have seen the demo example 'WDR_TEST_EVENTS' provided by SAP.

I have created the layout with one 'dropdownboxbyidx', one Table, a context with node dropdown1, child node table1 with attributes, and with the corresponding supply functions.

When I test this application initially, I got the values when I selected another value in the drop down. It is not changing the values in the table, but gives the error as "Access via null object reference not possible".

How can I resolve this problem?

I have written the following code in 'onselect':

```
method ONACTIONONSELECT .
wd_this->all_in_one_util->on_element_event( wdevent
).
endmethod.

I declared attribute 'ALL_IN_ONE_UTIL' with reference
type 'CL_WDR_ALL_IN_ONE_UTIL'.
```

I am getting the values in the listbox, but when I select the particular value in the list, the table is not changing as per selected value. That means 'Filltable1' supply function is not working.

The code for the Filltable1 supply function:

```
data:
lt_attributes type standard table of
if_mainview=>element_table1,
wa_attributes like line of lt_attributes,
carrid type s_carr_id,
lt_scarplan type cl_wd_flight_model=>tt_scarplan.
```

```
field-symbols:
<scarplan> like line of lt_scarplan.

parent_element->get_attribute( exporting name =
'CARRID' importing value = carrid ).
cl_wd_flight_model=>get_scarplan_by_carrid( exporting
i_carrid = carrid importing et_scarplan = lt_scarplan
).
loop at lt_scarplan assigning <scarplan>.
move-corresponding <scarplan> to wa_attributes.
insert wa_attributes into table lt_attributes.
endloop.
node->bind_elements( lt_attributes ).
```

When I click another value in the list, it's giving the following error 'Access via null object reference is not possible'.

How can I display the table data according to the selected value?

What should I write in the method 'ONACTIONONSELECT', instead of the following code:

```
"wd_this->all_in_one_util->on_element_event( wdevent
)".
```

A: For the changed values not coming in your table, check if you have done 'bind_elements' or 'bind_table' in the 'on_select' event handler. You need to bind every time.

If the user selects en entry and you update a table with elements regarding the selected value, then you have to get the selected element via the lead selection, or by using the 'wdevent' object passed to the action handler.

Then, read the selected value from the element, perform a selection, and add the result to the node of the table that should display the result.

Another suggestion is instead of a supply function, you can fill the value in 'ONSELECT' method of the dropdown.

The supply function will be called only when the table is filled for the first time. If you want it to be called everytime when the drop down changes, do a "node->invalidate( )" in the "on_select" event. Then, it will be forced to be called again.

Supply methods are normally called only once during initialization, depending on your context structure. So when you select another element, the supply method will not be called again.

One exception: If you will declare the node that contains the data for the table, as subnode of the node that contains the elements for the drop down and you declare this node as singleton, the supply method is called each time you select an element of the parent node.

So, you should use a method to fill it which you call in the action handler.

Write the code of the supply function in the 'onselect' and it should work fine. Don't forget to bind the table.

As suggested, you can use the code of the supply method with the exception that you have to get the context which is bound to the table manually. This can be done by using the wizard (Read Context).

Then, you have the reference of the node.

Question 26: Creating a Tray dynamically

I tried to develop a method where I can create a tray dynamically. I have embedded this code in the method 'WDDOINIT' of my View called 'MAIN_VIEW'. My longer term plan is to create x number of trays, where x is dictated by the number of entries in an Internal Table.

The code I have written compiles, but nothing appears where I thought it would.

```
create object wd_this->all_in_one_util.

data: node_input type REF TO if_wd_context_node,
elem_input TYPE REF TO if_wd_context_element,
stru_input type if_main_view=>element_input.

data: lr_view type ref to cl_wdr_view,
lr_tray type REF TO CL_WD_TRAY,
tray_id type string,
lr_caption type ref to cl_wd_caption,
caption_id type string,
lr_grid_data type ref to cl_wd_grid_data,
lr_grid_layout type ref to cl_wd_grid_layout.


*Navigate from <CONTEXT> to <INPUT> via lead
selection
node_input = wd_context->get_child_node( name =
if_main_view=>wdctx_input ).

lr_tray = cl_wd_tray=>new_tray(
EXPANDED = ABAP_TRUE
ID = tray_id
VIEW = lr_view "'MAIN_VIEW'
WIDTH = '100%'
).

* set the caption of the tray
concatenate lr_tray->id '_HEADER' into caption_id.
lr_caption = cl_wd_caption=>new_caption(
id = caption_id
text = 'text goes here'
view = lr_view ).
lr_tray->set_header( lr_caption ).

* create the grid layout data for tray
lr_grid_data = cl_wd_grid_data=>new_grid_data(
lr_tray ).
```

```
* assign the layout data to the tray
lr_tray->set_layout_data( lr_grid_data ).

* create a new grid layout for the content of the
tray
lr_grid_layout = cl_wd_grid_layout=>new_grid_layout(
lr_tray ).

* assign the grid layout to the tray
lr_tray->set_layout( lr_grid_layout ).
```

What did I miss?

A: You have to add the tray to the view:

```
LR_CONTAINER type ref to CL_WD_UIELEMENT_CONTAINER.


LR_CONTAINER ?= view->GET_ELEMENT(
'ROOTUIELEMENTCONTAINER' ).
LR_CONTAINER->ADD_CHILD( LR_tray ).
```

If we have to do any dynamic programming in web dynpro (creating UI elements dynamically), 'WDDOMODIFYVIEW' is the method where we need to code the logic for creating the tray.

But you have done the coding of creating tray in 'WDDOINIT', that's why it is not working fine. Just have the same code in 'WDDODMODIFYVIEW' and you need to have the below code to add this tray to view's 'ROOTUICONTAINER'.

```
data: lr_container TYPE REF TO
cl_wd_uielement_container.
lr_container ?= view->get_element(
'ROOTUIELEMENTCONTAINER' ).
" View is import parameter of wddomodifyview method.

lr_container->add_child( '' pass the tray that is
created ' ).
```

This is the way to create dynamic UI elements in web dynpro using 'wddodmodifyview'.

Question 27: Field Symbols

I am creating a structure and a table dynamically as shown below:

```
**filed symbols
FIELD-SYMBOLS: <table> TYPE table,
<row> TYPE data.


struct_type = cl_abap_structdescr=>create( comp_tab
).

struct_type = node_info->get_static_attributes_type(
).

table_type = cl_abap_tabledescr=>create( p_line_type
= struct_type ).

CREATE DATA my_table TYPE HANDLE table_type.
ASSIGN my_table->* TO <table>.

CREATE DATA my_row TYPE HANDLE struct_type.
ASSIGN my_row->* TO <row>.
```

Now in runtime, I would be able to see the structure of <table> and <row>, and also the data if it has any.

How would I read that data in to an internal table?

For example, if the table has a structure of 5 columns, how would I read 5th column?

I would like to overwrite the content of the 5th column with the content of the 4th column.

Is it possible? If it is, then how?

If you could see the field symbol declaration in your code, it's a type of some structure. But in my case, it is just <row> type data, and <table> type table.

When I say <row>-cloumn5, it's giving an error saying <row> is not of type structure.

What's the solution for this?

Lastly, is there any way we can assign the column5 value to <row> itself, so that we can modify <table > from <row>?

A: You can refer to the following code snippet:

Code:

```
************************************************************
method FILL_PLANT .


types : begin of str_cost,
kostl type zcostcenter-kostl ,
end of str_cost.


types : begin of str_ekgrp,
ekgrp type zekgrp-ekgrp,
end of str_ekgrp.


data : itab_cost type table of str_cost with default
key .
data : itab_ekgrp type table of str_ekgrp with
default key.
data : wa_mara type str_cost.
data : lt_attributes type
If_Request_Ior=>Elements_Plantnode,
wa_attributes type If_Request_Ior=>Element_Plantnode.

field-symbols : <fs_cost> type str_cost.

CALL FUNCTION 'ZPD_RFC_COSTCENTER' DESTINATION
'tr3_clnt800'
TABLES IT_COST = itab_cost.
*
CALL FUNCTION 'ZPD_RFC_PURGROUP' DESTINATION
'tr3_clnt800'
TABLES IT_EKGRP = itab_ekgrp .


loop at itab_cost assigning <fs_cost> .

wa_attributes-plant = <fs_cost>-kostl.
insert wa_attributes into table lt_attributes.

endloop.

node->bind_elements( lt_attributes ).
```

```
endmethod.
```

If you specify the addition STRUCTURE instead of typing for a field symbol, and 'struc' is a local program structure (a data object, not a data type) or a flat structure from the ABAP Dictionary, this structure is cast for the field symbol <fs>. You have to specify a data object 'dobj' that is initially assigned to the field symbol.

The field symbol copies the technical attributes of the structure 'struc' as if it were completely typed. When you assign a data object using the addition DEFAULT, or later using ASSIGN, its complete data type is not checked in non- Unicode programs. Instead, the system merely checks whether it has at least the length of the structure and its alignment.

In Unicode programs, we differentiate between structured and elementary data objects. For a structured data object 'dobj', its Unicode fragment view has to match the one of 'struc'. In the case of an elementary data object, the object must be character-type and flat, and 'struc' must be purely character-type. The same applies to assignments of data objects to field symbols typed using STRUCTURE when using the ASSIGN statement.

Field symbols declared using the addition STRUCTURE are a mixture of typed field symbols and a utility for casting structured data types. You should use the additions TYPE or LIKE for the FIELD-SYMBOLS statement to type field symbols, while the addition CASTING of the ASSIGN statement is used for casting.

This is the example:

```
DATA wa2 TYPE c LENGTH 512.
FIELD-SYMBOLS <scarr2> TYPE scarr.
ASSIGN wa2 TO <scarr2> CASTING.
<scarr2>-carrid = '...'.
```

You can also try the following code:

```
field-symbols : <data1> type any,
<data2> type any.

In the loop like
loop at <table> into <row>.
write the following code.
ASSIGN COMPONENT 5 of <row> to <data1>.
ASSIGN COMPONENT 4 of <row> to <data2>.
<data1> = <data2> .
modify statement for the table.

Endloop.
```

In the loop, you will get index 'sy-index' write

```
modify <table> index sy-tabix from <row> transporting
<data2>
```

Lastly, you have to pass the name of the field name, not the value i.e <data2>.

So create a variable of type string say 'lv_string'.

```
lv_string = name_of_column .
```

Then, after transporting write (lv_string)

like this:

```
modify <table> index sy-index from <row> transporting
(lv_string).
```

Question 28: Pop-up for file download

I'm trying to create a pop-up for file selection for download. Basically, I want to call:

call method cl_gui_frontend_services=>file_open_dialog

This works fine from a report, but from my web dynpro I get a dump because apparently there is no GUI (parameters www_active and activeX are all empty).

Does this method work with web dynpro at all?

Is there some other CL_WD* class for this purpose?

Are my system settings screwed up?

A: You should use the UIelement: filedownload (standard simple) of upload for those purposes. Depending on the target of the file transfer, use the "wdr_test_ui_elements" to get into the detail example.

Question 29: Add a drop down box in an ALV toolbar

I have a requirement where I need to add a drop down box in my ALV Toolbar. To be precise, it's next to the export button in my ALV.

How can I accomplish this?

It comes up with the following error message:

Method WDDOINIT
Field "R_TABLE" is unknown.

It is neither in one of the specified tables nor defined by a "DATA" statement.

How can I proceed further?

A: You can try the following code:

Adding the DropDown list to the ALV toolbar:

```
lr_functions ?= wd_this->r_table.

lr_function = lr_functions->create_function(
'MYDROPDOWNBYINDEX' ).
create object lr_dropdown_by_idx
exporting
texts_elementname = 'DROPDOWNBYINDEX.VALUE'.
lr_dropdown_by_idx->set_label_text(
'MYDROPDOWNBYINDEX' ).
lr_function->set_editor( lr_dropdown_by_idx ).
```

Providing the values to that DropDown:

Here in my example, 'DROPDOWNBYINDEX.VALUE' is the context attrubute. I wrote the Supply function for that node as follows:

```
data:
lt_dropdownbyindex type
if_componentcontroller=>elements_dropdownbyindex,
ls_dropdownbyindex type
```

```
if_componentcontroller=>element_dropdownbyindex.

ls_dropdownbyindex-value = 'Nothing'. "#EC NOTEXT
append ls_dropdownbyindex to lt_dropdownbyindex.

ls_dropdownbyindex-value = 'ActionDropdownByIndex'.
"#EC NOTEXT
append ls_dropdownbyindex to lt_dropdownbyindex.

node->bind_table( lt_dropdownbyindex ).
```

For reference, you can refer the WD component
'SALV_WD_TEST_TABLE_TOOLBR' which holds the same
code.

The 'r_table' reference is missing in your attributes of the view.

But you do not need it. 'e_table' seems to be the model of the
ALV which can be retrieved from the interface controller of the
ALV component. Just declare the controller usage in the
properties tab of your view.

Then, you can use the wizard to create the method call which
would look like this:

```
lr_ref_cmp_usage =   wd_this->wd_cpuse_alv( ).
    IF lr_ref_cmp_usage->has_active_component( ) IS
INITIAL.
      lr_ref_cmp_usage->create_component( ).
    ENDIF.

    lr_ref_if_contrl =   wd_this->wd_cpifc_alv( ).
```

Then, you can use the 'lr_ref_if_contrl' like
the 'r_table' reference:

```
lr_functions ?= lr_ref_if_contrl->get_model( ).
```

Another suggestion is to refer the WD Component
'SALV_WD_TEST_TABLE_TOOLBR' which will explain more
clearly the Toolbar concepts.
The 'R_TABLE' attribute can be created in the Component
controller. That's why it is asking you if it is unknown. So you can
access this variable in View using default attrubutes

'wd_comp_controller', or you do the ALV related coding in the respective view also instead of doing the code in the component controller.

Declaring the Flow & Behavior of the application

Question 30: Item selection between two lists

How can I realize a screen with two item lists, and between these two lists I need a button which moves one or more item from list1 to list2 and a second button which removes one or more item from list2 back to list one?

I've seen something like this for ALV settings in an ALV demo video.

Is there any WDA example, where I can see the UI elements that I need, including event handling, etc?

How do I get the selected entries with multiple selection possible?

A: You can create two context nodes, one to bind to the list of elements and the other to bind the list of selected elements. Have two internal tables and bind them to the context nodes. Then, have a button "Move" or something in between the lists. In the "On Action" of the button, in your event handler, remove the selected entry from the first table and append it to the internal table of the second table. Do a "bind_elements" on both nodes after that and the values will be refreshed?

In the event handler, you can get the lead selection index of the first node, which will give you the row that has been selected. Delete this row from the first internal table and append it to the second internal table.

You can try to have a look at the following web dynpro component: "WDR_TEST_UI_ELEMENTS".
It contains many examples of using various UI elements.

If both lists are of the same structure, then it will be very easy. Just create two nodes with this structure and bind it to the tables. Create the buttons and add actions to the buttons.

In the action, get the reference of the corresponding node and use "get_element( )" if only one element can be selected, or

"get_elements( )" if multi selection is allowed.
Then, get the reference to the other node and use
"bind_elements( )" to append the elements.

Afterwards, remove the elements from the first node:

In here, the user profiles is moved from one table to another.

```
METHOD onactionadd_profiles .
  DATA:
          lr_node_user_profiles          TYPE REF TO
if_wd_context_node,
          lr_node_profiles               TYPE REF TO
if_wd_context_node,
          lr_elem_profiles               TYPE REF TO
if_wd_context_element.

  data:
          lt_sel_profiles                type
WDR_CONTEXT_ELEMENT_SET,
          lt_profiles                    type table of
zsalsa_profile.

  data:
          ls_profile                     type
zsalsa_profile.


  lr_node_profiles = wd_context->get_child_node( name
= wd_this->wdctx_profiles ).
  lr_node_user_profiles = wd_context->get_child_node(
name = wd_this->wdctx_user_profiles ).

* get all selected profiles
  lt_sel_profiles = lr_node_profiles-
>get_selected_elements( abap_true ).

* build profile table and remove selected profiles
from node
  loop at lt_sel_profiles into lr_elem_profiles.
    lr_elem_profiles->get_static_attributes(
      importing
        static_attributes = ls_profile
    ).
    lr_node_profiles->remove_element(
lr_elem_profiles ).
    append ls_profile to lt_profiles.
  endloop.

* add selected profiles to user profiles.
  lr_node_user_profiles->bind_table(
    NEW_ITEMS = lt_profiles
    SET_INITIAL_ELEMENTS = abap_false
```

```
  ) .

endmethod.
```

Your screen layout will be a grid layout with colcount = 3, so that the two tables and the button in between all come in the same line.

You can use a normal table itself. It is important that the selection property of your context is set to '0..n' if you want multiple selection. If not, it will dump.

You can get the selected elements as "node->get_selected_elements()" that will return you a set of elements.

Question 31: Manual selection change behavior for tab strips

I have a web dynpro for abap application that contains a tab strip. This tab strip contains multiple tabs with ALV grids imbedded where users can enter information. I am using the data check method to catch and validate entries upon enter or action. If the user changes a cell and changes tabs without pressing enter or some other function, the changes are not validated. I know you can use the "onSelect" event to validate this data and then manually call the selected tab; I'm just not sure how to implement it.

How can I accomplish that?

A: You can try the following suggestion:

In the action handler method of Tab Strip, you can get the new tab id using the importing parameter "io_wdevent" as follows:

io_wdevent->get_string('TAB') ---> returns the new tab that is selected.
io_wdevent->get_string('OLD_TAB') ---> returns previous tab from which the new tab was selected.

Depending on the old tab, you can do the validation logic as you want.

Additional information on writing the validation logic in the "WDDOBEFOREACTION" method, if it works for you then it would be the best option to have the validation logic.

You can also try another suggestion as follows:

You can have a context attribute that holds the name of the currently selected tab. In the "OnSelect" method, read the context of your ALV (which will already have the changed values bound). Depending on that, set the context attribute "selected_tab" to whichever tab you wish to navigate. In the "modifyview" method, get the reference of your tab strip and set the selected tab manually.

Your code in the 'On Select' will be to read context, validate, and set the selected tab attribute to the name (ID) of the tab you have specified in the design time.

In the modify view, do the following:

```
data: lr_tabstrip type ref to cl_wd_tabstrip,
lr_context type ref to cl_wd_context_element,
lv_seltab type string.

lr_tabstrip ?= view->get_element( 'TABSTRIP' ).
lr_context = wd_context->get_element( ).
lr_context->get_attribute(
exporting
name = 'SELECTED_TAB'
importing
value = lv_seltab ).

lr_tabstrip->set_selected_tab( lv_seltab ).
```

Question 32: Service call via RFC

I am currently starting with WDA and I'm facing some problems in calling BAPI via RFC.

We have a "plain" WAS without SD or other modules. Our data is distributed over multiple R/3 systems.

When I try to implement a Service Call to the "BAPI BAPI_CUSTOMER_GETLIST" via RFC, I got the error message that this FM is not available in the current system (WAS).

I tried generating the call with the WIZARD. I guess when I tried to implement the service call by hand, it would work. Anyway, the main question is how this is handled in the best way. For example, how to handle missing structures or how to handle an upcoming updates on the back ends so that eventually the structures or FM parameters are changing.

How can I get this working?

What is the best practice on the following:
- Building wrapper on WAS which calls the FM via RFC on the other system?
- Installing missing modules on WAS?

What are the best practices to handle RFC's to an R/3 system when all the BAPI's and structures/tables which are needed to call the BAPI are only available on the R/3.

- Install missing packages on WAS?
- Transport structures to WAS?
- Define structures on WAS?

A: Prerequisite for using service call wizard is that the function module or in your case BAPI has to exit in the system.

I also assume you refer to the Service Call Wizard in the WD Explorer of SE80. This wizard generates the pure invocation as you will do in your coding too. The only difference is that you get a (a little bit bulky) context definition granted for free.

Maybe your RFC Destination or some other argument is not valid. Try to check the invocation within WD in the debugger, and later use the exact same arguments in test mode within se37.

If you do not have RFC in the WAS in which you have Web Dynpro ABAP but you need to call a RFC which resides in the different WAS, you can call a RFC using the keyword "Destination". All you have to do is to create a RFC Destination where your RFC exist using TCode sm59. Then, when you are calling the RFC just follow the following example:

```
CALL FUNCTION func DESTINATION dest
          parameter_list.
```

If WAS doesn't have the structure or BAPI, I think the best practice would be to check the support package. If there is a support package available which has the entire component you need, I would take this way.

Second would be transport to WAS, but not creating Object in WAS because you would have difficulties to track on this.

The last suggestion is try to define an http destination for the logical port of the service in the transaction "LPCONFIG" and a RFC-connection of type G in SM59.

Question 33: Error in the browser

The following is my code:

```
method ONACTIONCLICK .

data:
Node_Adobe_Data type ref to If_Wd_Context_Node,
Elem_Adobe_Data type ref to If_Wd_Context_Element,
Stru_Adobe_Data type
If_Z_Test3_View=>Element_Adobe_Data .
* navigate from <CONTEXT> to <ADOBE_DATA> via lead
selection
Node_Adobe_Data = wd_Context->get_Child_Node( Name =
IF_Z_TEST3_VIEW=>wdctx_Adobe_Data ).

* get element via lead selection
Elem_Adobe_Data = Node_Adobe_Data->get_Element( ).


data:

Item_IN like Stru_Adobe_Data-IN.

data:

Item_OUT like Stru_Adobe_Data-OUT.

* get single attribute
Elem_Adobe_Data->get_Attribute(
exporting
Name = `IN`
importing
Value = Item_In ).

call function 'CONVERSION_EXIT_ALPHA_OUTPUT'

exporting

in = ITEM_IN
importing

out = Item_out.


* navigate from <CONTEXT> to <ADOBE_DATA> via lead
selection
Node_Adobe_Data = wd_Context->get_Child_Node( Name =
IF_Z_TEST3_VIEW=>wdctx_Adobe_Data ).

* get element via lead selection
Elem_Adobe_Data = Node_Adobe_Data->get_Element( ).
```

```
* get single attribute
Elem_Adobe_Data->set_Attribute(
exporting
Name = `OUT`
Value = Item_Out ).

endmethod.
```

The error in the browser is the following:

```
Note

The following error text was processed in the system
SMT : Function parameter "IN" is unknown.
The error occurred on the application server
MD1AS086_SMT_01 and in the work process 0.
The termination type was: RABAX_STATE
The ABAP call stack was:
Method: ONACTIONCLICK of program
/1BCWDY/8ZTW4TLW2H1HI865VH9F==CP
Method: IF_WDR_VIEW_DELEGATE~WD_INVOKE_EVENT_HANDLER
of program /1BCWDY/8ZTW4TLW2H1HI865VH9F==CP
Method: INVOKE_EVENTHANDLER of program
CL_WDR_DELEGATING_VIEW========CP
Method: IF_WDR_ACTION~FIRE of program
CL_WDR_ACTION=================CP
Method: DO_HANDLE_ACTION_EVENT of program
CL_WDR_WINDOW_PHASE_MODEL=====CP
Method: PROCESS_REQUEST of program
CL_WDR_WINDOW_PHASE_MODEL=====CP
Method: PROCESS_REQUEST of program
CL_WDR_WINDOW=================CP
Method: EXECUTE of program
CL_WDR_MAIN_TASK==============CP
Method: IF_HTTP_EXTENSION~HANDLE_REQUEST of program
CL_WDR_MAIN_TASK==============CP
Method: EXECUTE_REQUEST_FROM_MEMORY of program
CL_HTTP_SERVER================CP
==========================================================
===
```

There are no syntax errors. Actually, in here IN is my attribute name. I also tried by declaring as DATA: IN type numc10. I still have the same problem.

How can I fix it?

A: You can try to debug your program and see on which line exactly you get the dump. Check if it is when you pull down the data from the context attribute, or when calling the "CONVERSION_EXIT_ALPHA_OUTPUT" function?

I guess your 'IN' context element was bound to an entry field, make sure it's not empty when you're running your WD.

Another analysis is that the parameters of the function module "CONVERSION_EXIT_ALPHA_OUTPUT" are input and output, not in and out as you have specified.

Try to use the pattern feature to generate the function call.

I also think te function parameters are wrong:

```
FUNCTION CONVERSION_EXIT_ALPHA_OUTPUT.
*"----------------------------------------------------
*"*"Lokale Schnittstelle:
*"  IMPORTING
*"     VALUE(INPUT) TYPE CLIKE
*"  EXPORTING
*"     VALUE(OUTPUT) TYPE CLIKE
*"----------------------------------------------------
```

In the function module there is no parameter called IN, it's INPUT and OUTPUT. But whereas in your code, you mentioned these as IN and OUT which is wrong.

Question 36: Getting a singleton component

I am developing a multi-component application. I have a model component which is the model of my MVC and is created from my main component.

I have other components which are loaded dynamically at runtime and which also defines a usage to this model component. The use of my model component is only relevant to the application if this component is a singleton in my work process.

Is there a built-in way to get a list of instances of a component usage within my work process?

How can I share "component instances" (of a usage which points to the same class or interface) between components?

My original idea was to use a normal ABAP class with the singleton DP.

But I have seen people writing model components and using special magic with the 'USAGE_MODEL' definition which seems to have its own way to be dealt with.

I had a look into "IF_WD_COMPONENT_USAGE~CREATE_COMPONENT" method, then I see "MODEL_USAGE TYPE REF TO IF_WD_COMPONENT_USAGE OPTIONAL".

Which would be the best way or the WD4A way?

A: It is possible to pass the reference of the usage from your main component which controls everything to all other components that have a usage of the same component.

All your components should have a 'set_usage' method which takes the reference to the usage. Your main component then can call this method and pass the reference.

In the implementation of this method in all the other components, do the following:

```
data:
        lr_usage      type if_wd_component_usage.

lr_usage = wd_this->cpuse_usage_name_of_usage( ).
lr_usage->enter_referencing_mode(
lr_usage_refrence_from_main_component ).
```

On the other hand, others do not recommend using components as model. Just create a normal
class or set of classes which reflect your model and build it as singleton. Then, you can access it from each component. It might be easier.

Another way would be to inject the model class to all other components via a set method in the component interface. So the main component would initially create the model and pass it to all other components via their interface controllers.

There is another way to transfer the reference of the usage to a used component.

If you define a component usage of the type of your 'model_component' in the target component (which should use the same reference) and you name this usage "MODEL_USAGE", you can transfer your model component usage via the "create_component" method.

Example:

```
data:
        lr_model_comp_usage     type ref to
if_wd_component_usage,
        lr_modeluser_comp       type ref to
if_wd_comp_usage.

lr_model_comp_usage = wd_this-
>wd_cpuse_usage_modelcomp( ).
if lr_model_comp_usage->has_active_component( ) is
initial.
    lr_model_comp_usage->create_component( ).
endif.

lr_modeluser_comp = wd_this-
>wd_cpuse_usage_modelusercomp( ).
```

```
if lr_modeluser_comp->has_active_component( ) is
initial.
    lr_modeluser_comp->create_component( model_usage =
lr_model_comp_usage ).
endif.
```

Question 37: Using only one view from a component

I have a component C1 with 7 views. I have another component C2 in which I want to use only 1 view of the component C1 rather than the entire component.

How can I do that?

A: I suppose that a view is created by the creation of the entire component.

Views are used by windows to determine the navigation logic. Thus, if you want to only use one view then you need to change the logic of your window, or create another one with its own navigation flow.

So I would recommend you to create a new window (whit its own navigation) in C1 which would reuse the sole view that you need.

You can also try the following solution steps:

1. Add a "ViewUIContainerElement" to your view in C2.
2. Insert the view to the window of C2 and go to the window.
3. Here, open the node of your view and you will see the "ViewUIContainerELement".
4. Right click on that element and choose Embed View.

But you have to define the component usage of C1 before you can select views of C1 here.

Question 38: Cardinality: automatic creation of initial elements

As far as I know, the systems automatically creates elements when the cardinality is '1..1' or '1..n'. Now, I would like to know when exactly the system does this creation of initial elements.

One of my context nodes has a cardinality of '1...1'. In some cases, I can't set the attributes because there is no element. Therefore, I want to have a better understanding of when the system creates initial elements.

My SUPPLY function checks whether there is an element (among other things). If not, it creates one.

But then the program dumps in
"CL_WDR_VIEW_ELEMENT_ADAPTER->GET_ATTRIBUTE_EXTERNAL"
because "ATTRIBUTE-ELEMENT" is initial (it is about the node to which the SUPPLY function is assigned).

A: The element will be created in the moment the context is initialized.

I would say that the context is initialized when the component is created. Before any view, 'view controller' or 'view context' is created.

A context element is created automatically, if:

- it is declared with cardinality 1..1 or 1..n and
- there is no supply function declared for this node.

If a supply function is declared, it has to make sure that the cardinality is fulfilled.

The creation of the first element is done at the same time as the supply function would be called, if there were any.

This means that as soon as you access the element (e.g. by reading or writing any of its attributes) the element is created.

So, there should be no need for you to worry about the time, at which the element is created.
I assume that the element is not created, because you have declared a supply function.

There is no need to check whether there is an element in the supply function. If the supply function is called, there IS NO element in the node.

Please check the exception raised in the adapter. You'll find the text rather at the beginning of the dump display. Perhaps the lead selection is not set.

Question 39: Nested tables in PDF

I am using transaction SFP, and I want to create a table in the PDF in which I use 2 different data tables.

The table contents are like this:

Table 1:

```
A  1  2  3  4  5
A  1  2  3  4  6
B  1  2  3  4  5
B  1  2  3  4  6
```

Table 2

```
A  7  8  9
B  7  8  9
```

The result I am looking for is:

```
A  7  8  9
A  1  2  3  4  5
A  1  2  3  4  6
B  7  8  9
B  1  2  3  4  5
B  1  2  3  4  6
```

I have created the table with two different lines, but the result I obtained was:

```
A  1  2  3  4  5
A  1  2  3  4  6
B  1  2  3  4  5
B  1  2  3  4  6
A  7  8  9
B  7  8  9
```

How can I achieve the result that I want?

A: I assume that you would have created the form in SFP and you would have embedded the form in the UI element interactive form UI element in the WD component.

Actually, this is the issue with the WD i.e. if you have a nested nodes context in form. But if we see the context generated once, we embed the form to interactive form. The context generated in the WD component will have 2 separate nodes, instead of the nested nodes. Hence, the linear output comes in the result.

I had a similar issue and resolved by calling the FM's and generated the spool, and read the spool then display the output in the PDF in WD abap.

Question 40: Identify the row number when a button is clicked in a table

I would like to use a button in the table column.

In this case, how would I identify the row number when the user clicks the button?

Is clicking the button affects the context change log?

A: If you want to know the row number, in the 'action' there is a parameter "WDEVENT" which gives the complete row where you clicked.

In "WDEVENT", you have "GET_CONTEXT_ELEMENT" method as well as "GET_DATA" method to fetch the data and it doesn't require any lead selection.

If it is an ALV table, then you need to get the selected row from "r_param->index of the event handler" 'ON_CLICK'.

Another way is in your button's event handler, call the method 'wdevent->get_context_element' ('CONTEXT_ELEMENT'), which will return you the element where the button was clicked. Do a "get_static_attributes" to get the row data. I dont think the context change log will be updated on a button click.

Question 41: Check which button were pressed

I want to check which button the user pressed.

I do this:

```
DATA:
LR_VIEW_CONTROLLER TYPE REF TO IF_WD_VIEW_CONTROLLER,
LF_ACTION TYPE REF TO IF_WD_ACTION.

LR_VIEW_CONTROLLER ?= wd_this->wd_get_api( ).
CALL METHOD LR_VIEW_CONTROLLER->GET_CURRENT_ACTION
RECEIVING
RESULT = LF_ACTION.

IF LF_ACTION->NAME = 'GO'.
* do something
ENDIF.
```

It's ok. But when the user pressed the no button, then it gets dump:

Access via 'NULL' object reference not possible.

The problem is: LF_ACTION->NAME is initial.

Is there any other way to check this?

I know this:

```
data: lv_event_name type string.
lv_event_name = wdevent->get_name( ).
```

The problem here is it goes only in the 'event-handler-method'.

A: To avoid the error, put all your code inside:

```
if lf_action is not initial.
endif.
```

You can also try the following:

```
IF LF_ACTION IS INITIAL.
* some action
ENDIF.
```

Question 42: Clear message log

My code displays the message but when the area is empty, it displays **'No Message'**.

How can I hide it?

I even applied "Clear_Messages".

```
CALL METHOD l_current_controller->get_message_manager
RECEIVING
message_manager = l_message_manager.

l_message_manager->clear_messages( ).

CALL METHOD l_message_manager->report_t100_message
EXPORTING
msgid = 'ZHRM_PZ28'
msgno = msg_val
msgty = msg_typ.
```

A: Check how your WDA (Web Dynpro Application) is set.

Also have a look via SE80 to the properties of your WDA. You should find an area called "Handling of message", try changing the setting.

Question 43: Reset selection in ALV

We have an ALV on a WD4A view which allows multiple lines to be selected.

How can I completely reset the selection when returning to this view?

So when I return to the view, I don't want the lines to be selected any longer.

How can this be done?

A: To remove all selections, just clear the context node which you have bounded to the ALV.

Sample code:

```
DATA:
node_objects_info TYPE REF TO if_wd_context_node,
elem_objects_info TYPE REF TO if_wd_context_element,
stru_objects_info TYPE wd_this->element_objects_info.

node_objects_info = wd_context->get_child_node( name
= wd_this->wdctx_objects_info ).

CALL METHOD node_objects_info->clear_selection.
```

Here, 'objects_info' is the node to which I have bound. Replace it with your node name.

Place the code above in the inbound handler method used to enter into the view where you want to unselect the rows.

Question 44: Window not visible

I am trying to create a new application in WebDynPro ABAP, but I didn't find a window to drag my newly created view into it.

What can be the solution?

A: Right click on your webdynpro component; create a window and embed your view into it. While creating your component, you would have probably missed specifying the window name.

Question 45: Setting several containers in the right position in one view

There are 3 UI controls in one view, on the left is a Tree and on its right, there is a group that contains several inputfileds. We need one ALV control to show just below this group and right to the Tree.

The root container is 'MatrixLayout', and the Tree is 'MatrixHeadLayout'. The group is 'MatrixData'.

How can I set the ALV container?

A: You can use transparent container and put your ALV container in it. Also, you can use another blank transparent container to cover up the space below tree. Here, you will have to do some trial and error in padding and moving your transparent container to right most position.

Another way is to make your "RootUIElementContainer" as Matrix Layout or even grid layout with column size 2. Now, put the group and your ALV control together in a transparent container. Make the layout for this container as Grid Layout with column size 1. So your tree will come to the left and both the other containers will be to your right.

You can make the "RootUIElementContainer" as grid layout with column size 2, and put the group and ALV control together in a transparent container1. Make the layout for this container as Grid Layout with column size 1.

Also, make the height as 100% for both your tree and the transparent container.

Question 46: Close a portal window through a button event within the WD-APP

When I click on a link within the enterprise portal environment, it opens a WD application within a pop-up (portal window). This application has a CANCEL button. When a user clicks on this, the portal window should close.

How can this be achieved?

I tried firing the outbound plug of type exit of the WD app main window, but it just blanks out the screen and doesn't close the window itself.

A: This is not standard functioality. There is a work around: You can create an HTML code page in SICF containing the following:

```
<html
><head>
<script language="JavaScript">
function closewindows()
{
window.close();
}
</script>
</head>
<body onload="closewindows()">
</body>
</html>
.
```

Check the test program in the WD component "wdr_test_window_suite".

Updating the script code:

```
<html><script> function closeWindow( ){ top.close( );
} </script><body><form>
```

In this case, the application was logged off successfully.
```
<input type="button" value="close window"
onclick="closeWindow( );" /><><></body></html>
```

in SICF - this will close the window.

Question 47: Retaining the text in "text edit" element

I have a requirement where I need to preserve the text in case the user has entered something.

As of now, it automatically gets converted into the upper case. E.g. the user enters "Hello World",it is getting saved as "HELLO WORLD". I don't want this case conversion to happen.

How can I fix this?

A: Your text edit is binded to some context attribute, and the attribute has some data type. You can save the data as lower case, which means the upper case conversion will not be done by checking the lower case property of the domain.

Create a domain with the data type you want. In the definition tab, set the lower case check box. Then, create a data element using this domain and use it.

Question 49: "WDDOMODIFYVIEW" error

I am one step further on that subject, but I have a follow up question related to the above mentioned method 'prepare_dynamic_navigation'.

I specified 'target_embedding_position' with the dynamically created view container (value = 'WS_CONFIG/SEC_SERV_VIEW_CONT'), but the static view is not displayed in the tab, i.e. the tab remains empty.

So I am missing something. I fired the navigation plug, but that leads in "WDDOMODIFYVIEW" to an error ("Navigation in Phase WDDOMODIFYVIEW Cannot Be Triggered"), so this is not the correct way.

How can I resolve this?

The firing of the plug remains a problem. I registered on the tabstrip an event for selecting a tab (via 'set_on_select'). When selected, that event handler fires the outbound plug to the static view. But when the tabstrip is displayed first, the static view is not visible until the tab gets manually selected in the tabstrip.

How can I display that view right at the first displaying of the tabstrip?

Or how can I fix the "fire plug" problem from above?

A: The view usage name is the name of the view suffixed with '_usage_1'.

E.g: if your static view name is 'V_STATIC', then the view usage name would be 'V_STATIC_USAGE_1'.

If you want to navigate to the view automatically, then use the method "do_dynamic_navigation". However, this shouldn't be used within the method "wddomodifyview( )".

If you are using "prepare_dynamic_navigation( )", then the

outbound plug needs to be fired explicitly.

Hence, you can save your view reference as a global attribute the first time the application is loaded, and later on use it in any method to create dynamic UI elements and finally call the method "do_dynamic_navigation". In this way, we wouldn't be doing navigation from within "wddomodifyview".

Maybe using the UI-Element **"HorizontalContextualPanel"** instead of the 'TabStrip-Control' can make life easier.

You can combine the UI-Element 'HorizontalContextualPanel' and a 'ViewContainer' for an application which needs to show a varying number of tabstrips.

A Web Dynpro Component Interface can be added to the 'ViewContainer'. The Web Dynpro Components shown in the 'ViewContainer' all implement the WD Component Interface.

During runtime, the components matching the active tabstrip are created.

DATA lr_cmp_usage TYPE REF TO if_wd_component_usage.
DATA l_component_name TYPE string.
lr_cmp_usage->create_component(l_component_name).

If you mean your first view (default without the navigation), you should check the window part of your component. Go to the 'viewcontainer' where this is happening and right click on the default view, then set as 'default'.

You can also set the default view usage for the dynamically created view container as follows:

In the scenario below, I have a view container 'vc2' and I am setting the default view usage dynamically. Perhaps you can use the same logic for your tabstrip implementation.

```
data:
lview type ref to cl_wdr_view,
uinfo type ref to if_wdr_rr_view_usage,
vca type ref to IF_WDR_RR_VIEW_CNT_ASSIGNMENT.

lview ?= view.
```

```
uinfo ?= lview->VIEW_USAGE_INFO.
vca = uinfo->GET_VCA_FOR_CONTAINER('VC2').

vca->set_default_view_usage('V_STEP1_USAGE_1').
```

Lastly, you can rebuild your WDC and enter static tabstrip elements which are completed by the dynamic ones.

All the static tabs, each of them planned to keep an already existing view should be defined as static, and bound on each of them an individual context element for its visibility setting.

Question 50: Logged user in Web Dynpro

How can I access the user loged in a webdynpro?

In this BAPI, it will use the SAP SSO or must I inform any import parameter to this works?

A: In Web Dynpro ABAP, you can always access the logged in user account ID via the system variable: SY-UNAME. To look-up the user account and read the full name, use the BAPI "BAPI_USER_GET_DETAIL". The information you want will be in the ADDRESS parameter.

Look at the signature on the BAPI, there is an importing parameter for username. This way you can look information on any user. However, if you want information on the currently logged in user, just pass in the 'sy-uname' to this parameter:

```
data return type standard table of bapiret2.
data ADDRESS TYPE  BAPIADDR3
call function 'BAPI_USER_GET_DETAIL'
  exporting
    username = sy-uname
  importing
    address  = address
  tables
    return   = return.
```

Question 51: Making transparent container visible or invisible by code

I want make transaparent container visible or invisible based some boolean value.

I have gone through class "CL_WD_UIELEMENT" and "CL_WD_TRANSPARENT_CONTAINER". I found method 'SET_VISIBLE'.

Suppose, let the name of my transperant container be 'TC_COSTCENTER'.

What code do I have to write? Where should I write?

I am writing it in the code 'WD_INIT' as this process is based on the value that I get on a boolean value which tells and decide on the visibility of the transparent container.

A: The easiest way is to bind the property 'Visible' to a boolean attribute of your context, and fill this attribute from ABAP as needed. Otherwise, you are going to use Dynamic Programming that is for WDA "experts".

The dynamic programming way is as follows:

First, you need to get a reference to the root element 'ROOTUIELEMENTCONTAINER' from the view reference available within the 'wddomodifyview' method. The variable returned is of type "cl_w_uielement_container". You can use the method "get_root_element( )" of the interface "if_wd_view" for this purpose.

Next, get a reference to the transparent container by using the method "get_child" of the class 'cl_wd_uielement_container' (using the variable returned from the previous call), and cast it to a variable of the class "cl_wd_transparent_container". To this method, you need to pass the id of your transparent container.

Once you have the reference, you can use the method "set_visible( )" to make the container visible or invisible at runtime.

However, you need to be careful about the placement of this code within the 'wddomodifyview' method because it would get executed every time. Thus, the best way is to store the reference to view in a component controller the first time and later on use this attribute anywhere within your component.

You can also accomplish this by setting the value of "WDUI_VISIBLITY" value as '01', or '02'.

Question 52: Syntax error

I get a statement "ENDMETHOD is missing" error in the following code:

```
method GET_BOOKINGS.

*------------------------------------------------------*
* CLASS zcl_wdabap_flight_model DEFINITION
*------------------------------------------------------*
*
*------------------------------------------------------*
CLASS zcl_wdabap_flight_model DEFINITION.
PUBLIC SECTION.
methods GET_BOOKINGS IMPORTING
carrid TYPE s_carrid
connid type s_connid
fldate type s_date
EXPORTING
bookings type TY_BOOKINGS.

ENDCLASS. "zcl_wdabap_flight_model DEFINITION

*------------------------------------------------------*
* CLASS zcl_wdabap_flight_model IMPLEMENTATION
*------------------------------------------------------*
*
*------------------------------------------------------*
CLASS zcl_wdabap_flight_model IMPLEMENTATION.
METHOD get_bookings.
select * from sbook into table bookings where
carrid = carrid and
connid = connid and
fldate = fldate.
ENDMETHOD. "get_bookings

ENDCLASS. "zcl_wdabap_flight_model IMPLEMENTATION

data:
Itab_Bookings type
IF_COMPONENTCONTROLLER=>Elements_Bookings,
Stru_Bookings like line of Itab_Bookings,
Stru_FlightList type
IF_COMPONENTCONTROLLER=>Element_Flight_List,
cl type ref to zcl_wdabap_flight_model.

parent_element->get_static_attributes( importing
static_attributes = Stru_FlightList ).

create object cl.

Itab_Bookings = call method cl->get_bookings (
exporting
```

```
carrid = Stru_FlightList-airlineid
connid = Stru_FlightList-connectid
fldate = Stru_FlightList-flightdate
importing
bookings = bookings ).

node->bind_table( Itab_Bookings ).

endmethod. "get_bookings
```

Where is the error?

Page 12 says I should create the class inside the 'get_bookings' method.

Both methods have the same name, but they have different visibility. One method is an instance method of the class I just defined, and it is called "call method <object instance>->get_bookings". The ABAP compiler should be able to figure out which method I intend to call, wouldn't it?

A: Your class definition and implementation are inside the method, end method statement. That could be the problem.

You're trying to call the same method that you are defining again. Always logically separate your code as declaration definition and implementation, and use pretty printer. This will help you identify these kinds of error much faster.

Normally, this error comes when there is no matching end method statement for a "method" statement.

On your second question, you do not need this class here.

You could add your method which selects all bookings inside the assistance class of your component.

Then, your code would look like the following:

```
wd_assist->get_bookeings( ... ).
```

The wording in the tutorial does indeed give that meaning. What it intends to convey, however, is different.

You can check if you have the 'class cl_wdabap_flight_model' in your system. In which case, if you copy paste the code in your supply function, it would work. If the class does not exist, then you create a 'Z class zcl_wdabap_flight_model' and indtroduce a static method 'get_bookings' that would return a table of type 'SBOOK'. You would just put the select query inside that method.

Question 53: Setting the main application's title

1. How can I set the default title displayed in the browser's title bar? Now, I can only see the name of the component and "[Web Dynpro for ABAP]". Where can I change that value?

2. Is it possible to change this title dynamically from within the application?

A: You can maintain it in the description field of the web dynpro application.

You can do this by creating a GUI title. Go into SE80 and enter your application program name. Now, right click on your program name in the left window and choose "Create -> GUI Titles". Enter a title code (the screen number) and title text. Then in the PBO module for your screen, you need to put this line:

```
SET TITLEBAR 'titlecode'.
```

"titlecode" is the screen number of your title text.

There's only uncertainty if you can change the value of the text dynamically.

Defining the data binding

Question 54: Show dynamically created HTML page from WD4A

I want to display some invoice data for a customer from a WD4A application. Therefore, I want to fetch the necessary data from SAP tables and show it in a nice format (HTML and CSS code) in a popup window. I don't need any buttons or other actions in this pop-up; I just want to display the raw data to an invoice-like format.

How I can do that?

A: You can dynamically create the UI elements using the UI element classes. You could also embed html pages using IFRAME. Pick the correct options.

Each UI Element has a corresponding class. For example, input field has "cl_wd_input_field" and so on. You can create references to these UI elements and do your context binding etc at runtime. If you have your context statically defined, you can use it to bind to your elements, or the context itself can be defined at runtime.

Create an empty view and call it as a popup view when you want to display these details. In the "modifyview" method of that view, add the UI elements you wish to add. This should be done in "modifyview" method only.

These are the available classes which can be used to create dynamic UI elements:

```
cl_wd_uielement_container,
cl_wd_input_field,
cl_wd_input_field,
cl_wd_dropdown_by_key,
cl_wd_radiobutton_group_by_key,
cl_wd_label,
cl_wd_label,
cl_wd_text_view,
cl_wd_text_view,
cl_wd_button,
cl_wd_button,
cl_wd_horizontal_gutter,
```

Question 55: Value Help in WD Table

I have a problem with value help in a Web Dynpro Table.

In my WD, I have a table with a field that has a free 'Value help'. If I press F4, the Value help is opening. If I select an item in the value of the Help, the pop-up is closing but the selected value is not in the table cell.

How can I solve this problem?

A: Check if you have implemented an event handler for the "VH_DATA_SELECTED "event. You should explicitly bind the selected value to your context over there, only then it would get displayed.

For free value help, you have to implement the data setting by your own.

There is no "WDEVENT" in the OVS callback, but you should have a deeper look at the attributes of the "OVS_CALLBACK_OBJECT". There you will find the reference to the element and the attribute name. Using this technique, you can also use one OVS component usage for different value helps.

For self implemented value help, you will also find the context element and the attribute in method "SET_VALUE_HELP_LISTENER" as an attribute of the passed listener.

Question 56: Standard Tables

I have a standard table in which I want to select 1 column. Is there any way I can recognize which column was been selected?

A: When you select the table column (TabelColumn Ui Element) in the view designer,
you can create an action for the "onAction" event of this column. But it seems that you have to create one handler per column so that you can find out which column was clicked.

The event is triggered when the user clicks the header of the column.

Another suggestion is that you can bind an action into the table column editor (input field and others). This will directly send you to an event handler in which you can process the selection.
E.g. in an input field, you can bind an action to toggling the enter button.

You can also build one action for all the columns and assign this action to all columns. In the action, you can find out which column was clicked as follows:

```
data:
        lv_col_id type string.
  lv_col_id = wdevent->get_string( 'ID' ).
```

lv_col_id is the ID of the selected column then.

If you know the ID of the column, you will know which attribute of the context node is bound to this column. Just get all the elements of the node and read the corresponding attribute of each element to get all data of the column.

On the other hand, in the Standard Table you don't have this automatic column select functionality. However, you can set "onAction" of Table Column to an event handler, and you can set a variable inside the event handler and in "WDMODIFYVIEW" you can use the code as follows to make that column as 'selected'.

```
data: lr_table type ref to cl_wd_table.
data: lr_tab_column type ref to cl_wd_table_column.

if <the column> selected.
lr_table ?= view->get_element( ID = 'TAB' ).
lr_tab_column = lr_table->get_column( ID =
'TAB_NACHN' ).
lr_tab_column->set_cell_design( value = '06' ).
endif.
```

By default, cell design will be '01' for columns. You can have different values for this cell design which you can find in "WDUI_TABLE_CELL_DESIGN" data element.

You can use the same event handler for all the columns inside the event handler
and take the ID and set it in context.

In "WDDOMODIFYVIEW", replace "TAB_NACHN" with the ID in the code.

Question 57: PDF doc error: filedownloadUI vs. cl_wd_runtimeservices=>attach_file_to

I need to download a PDF doc from DMS. I got the external BAPI call that returns the file binary data as array of 2550 length raw data ('x') type.

I converted this into XSTRING and used "filedownloadUI" to open it. It worked. However, the **following code**, attached to a button action, calling "attach_file_to_response" **does not work.**

```
   call method
cl_wd_runtime_services=>attach_file_to_response
    EXPORTING
      i_filename   = line_Filecontent_Node-filename
      i_content    = line_Filecontent_Node-filecontent
      i_mime_type  = line_Filecontent_Node-mimetype.
*     i_in_new_window = abap_true
*     i_inplace       = abap_false.
```

The following code, linked to "filedownloadUI" is working:

```
.........
types:   char3(3).
types:   char255(255).
data: dappl type char3.
data: filename type char255.
data: dms_content type table of YBAPI_DMSCONTENT
initial size 0.
field-symbols <content> like line of dms_content.
data: BIN_FILESIZE           TYPE      I.
types: field2550(2550) type x.
data: content_binary type table of field2550 initial
size 0.
field-symbols <content_binary_row> like line of
content_binary.
data: loopCount type i,
      xstringTab type table of xstring.
data xstringRow  type xstring.
data datastream  type xstring.

***** for xstring conversion ******
data conv_out type ref to cl_abap_conv_out_ce.
conv_out = cl_abap_conv_out_ce=>create( encoding =
'UTF-8' ).
```

```
loopCount = 0.
data: counter type i,
      xlen type i,
      totalRead type   i,
      remain2read type i.
loop at dms_content assigning <content>.
  bin_filesize = <content>-length.
  counter = <content>-counter.
  loopCount = loopCount + 1.
    xlen = 2550.
    at last.
      totalRead = ( loopCount - 1 ) * 2550.
      remain2read = <content>-length - totalRead.
      xlen = remain2read . "603.
    endat.
  conv_out->convert(
  exporting
    data = <content>-data(xlen)
  importing
    buffer = xstringRow ).
  append xstringRow to xstringTab.
endloop.
concatenate LINES OF xstringTab into datastream in
byte mode.

  Stru_Filecontent_Node-FILECONTENT = datastream.

  case dappl.
    when 'doc' or 'DOC'.
        Stru_Filecontent_Node-MIMETYPE =
'application/word'.
    when 'xls' or 'XLS'.
        Stru_Filecontent_Node-MIMETYPE =
'application/excel'.
    when  'pdf' or 'PDF'.
        Stru_Filecontent_Node-MIMETYPE =
'application/pdf'.
    when others.
        Stru_Filecontent_Node-MIMETYPE =
'plain/text'.
  endcase.
  node->bind_structure( Stru_Filecontent_Node ).
endmethod.
```

However, both segments of the code works for other types of file like office docs, tiff image, jpg, etc. It's only on PDF that we have a problem.

What can be the solution for this?

A: You can try to clear the buffer to make the function call work. Try to use the following:

```
clear: xstringtab, bin_filesize.
clear datastream.
```

Question 58: Calling R/3 Transaction from WDA

I have created an application with 1 View, which is empty. I have put this piece of code in the Init Method.

```
data l_componentcontroller type ref to
ig_componentcontroller .
data l_api_componentcontroller type ref to
if_wd_component.
data l_sapgui_manager type ref to
cl_wdr_sapgui_integration.

l_componentcontroller = wd_this-
>get_componentcontroller_ctr( ).
l_api_componentcontroller = l_componentcontroller-
>wd_get_api( ).
l_sapgui_manager = l_api_componentcontroller-
>get_sapgui_manager( ).


if l_sapgui_manager is not initial.
l_sapgui_manager->fire_start_transaction( transaction
= 'ZRUN' ).
endif.
```

When I run my application, nothing happens. It just shows the blank view and does not call the Transaction ZRUN.

What can be the problem?

A: The value of "l_sapgui_manager" is initial all the time.

```
l_componentcontroller->wd_get_api( ).

will not populate l_sapgui_manager .....
```

"sapgui_manager" will be populated only when you are calling a web dynpro application inside a SAP GUI. It means something like you will create a SAP GUI, and then you create a frame inside that and embed the web dynpro application inside that. If you are running the application through the browser, it will be always initial.

Question 59: Delete ALV WD settings

I have used the settings (Right mouse -> settings) of an ALVA WD to remove a column. This gave me a NULL reference exception. However, this is not my trouble.

My problem now is how to reset the ALV to all columns. Since I can not get back to the window, ("the null reference issue") I was not able to reset my settings in the browser.

Where are the settings stored so I can delete them?

A: This can be done with "wd_analyze_config_user"

```
<xx>/sap/bc/webdynpro/sap/wd_analyze_config_user;
```

Question 60: Transport Personalization

We figured out that we can personalize WD Screens. I am talking about the client wide customization.

How can we transport this customization once we have completed it on our development machine?

A: The Web Dynpro component is like any other ABAP development component, it simply uses the existing transport system, same as all other objects.

The code wizard is the icon which looks like a magic wand. The code wizard will fire when you click that icon.

We do it with component and application configurations now, this way we can transport it.

Question 61: Display sample ABAP list

What is the best practice to display an abaplist returned from memory using
submit report?

I tried converting to text and use the 'textview', but I was not able to add the line breaks
so the format looks bad.

A: You can try the formatted text view. Check if it is already available in your system. Just separate the lines with " ". Otherwise, you can use the 'textedit' in a read-only state and the context attribute is a 'string_table'.

Question 62: Have an UI Element to display abaplist

I already tried the 'FormattedTextView' but it seems that it can not handle larger
texts because I get an error: "Regular Expression is to complex".

I just added all the line of the result to one string and mapped it to the UI Element. However, when I shorten the string, it gets displayed but does not look good enough.

I will try to run the report as service and convert the output to HTML which I attach
to the response and display it in an IFRAME.

It would be nice to have an UI Element to display abaplist. Is this possible?

A: I also use BSPs or Services to render ABAPs are Simple HTML lists. No interactive stuff, just simple Html, but it works and is easy. Your IFRAME can call a simple Service or BSP for example... see below regards Phil. [code] method IF_HTTP_EXTENSION~HANDLE_REQUEST.

```
* This piece of code is a generic OUTPUT in
* HTML format, of ABAP LISTs.
* ALV NOT SUPPORTED. Use ITS service for that.
* Variants also supported etc.
*
* HOW TO:
* create a class using interface IF_HTTP_EXTENSION
*Place this code in the HANDLE_REQUEST METHOD.
*create a new service in SICF entering your new class
*as the handler.

* Known Restrictions:
* NO CALL SCREENS etc that cause SAPGUI dialog.


* Nice test reports RSUSR003 or RSUSR005
data: lv_variant type char30.
data: lv_repname type sy-repid.
data: output_str type string.

data: html type table of w3html.
data: html_wa type w3html.
```

```
data: listobject type table of abaplist.


* to call
*http://host:port/this_service?report=rxxxxxxx&varian
t=vxxxxxxxx

lv_repname = server->request-
>get_form_field('report').
lv_variant = server->request-
>get_form_field('variant').

if lv_variant = space.
* the abap output section
submit (lv_repname) and return exporting list to
memory.
else.
submit (lv_repname) using selection-set lv_variant
and return exporting list to memory.

endif.
call function 'LIST_FROM_MEMORY'
tables
listobject = listobject.

call function 'WWW_HTML_FROM_LISTOBJECT'
exporting
report_name = lv_repname
tables
html = html
listobject = listobject.

clear output_str.
loop at html into html_wa.
concatenate output_str html_wa into output_str.
endloop.


call method server->response->set_cdata( data =
output_str ).

endmethod.
[/code]
```

Question 63: Outbound plug of a "view_container_uielement"

Is there any kind of "outbound plug" for a "view_container_uielement"?

I would like to detect when a view contained in a "view_container_uielement" has reached an outbound plug. This would then allow me to jump out of the view containing the container.

Does it sound reasonable? Is it possible?

A: There is no need to detect this. It is possible (and the framework is explicitly designed to support this) to create a navigation link from outbound plug of the inner view to an inbound plug of the view replacing the outer view.

Let's assume you have a window W with 2 views, V1 and V2. Inside of V1 there is another view VA. If you leave VA, you want to display V2 instead of V1. Right?

The hierarchy of the window should look like this:

```
W
\-V1
 \-Area1
  \-VA
   \- OUT_VA
\- V2
 \- IN_V2
```

Then, drag a navigation link from "V1*Area1*VA*OUT_VA" to "V2*IN_V2" and fire "OUT_VA".

Question 64: escape V1 completely

If I create a link from "VA-OUT_VA" to "V2-IN_V2", then I will get the following tree:

W
\-V1
\-Area1
\-v2

I want to escape V1 completely.

Is there another way to achieve the same?

Could it be possible to send an "event" from the inner view to the view containing the container (the outer view)?

So, this inner view would tell the outer view it is ready to call the outer view's outbound plug.

A: You should place V2 in your window at the same position as V1, not at the same position as the inner view.

Question 65: An indicative view

I also need something like an event from the container view to the upper view which would indicate that the upper view should go to V2.

How can I achieve this?

A: Just create an event in component controller of the inner view. Then if you want to
navigate from upper view to view2, fire the event in a method of the view controller of
the inner view. You can do this by using the wizard. You will find a fire_... method in the used component controller which has to be called.

Create an event handler for the event in the upper view, and in this handler fire the plug that navigates to view2.

Question 66: Definition of event

I am not sure where the event should be defined, whether inside the container view or upper view.

1. My wizard does not show any kind of fire method for the event I created which is quite strange. Can I call manually? What is the name convention?

2. Is the following sentence correct?

An event which is not handled in the local component can be handled by the component which is embedding one of its windows? Thus, should I define this event two times?

A: You should define the event on the component controller level of the component
which contains the view you use as inner view. Then you have to define the usage
of the component controller at the properties tab of this view. When you use the
wizard, just click on 'call' method of used controller -> select the component
controller -> use F4 and you will see all methods of the component controller.
There should be the fire method.

You also can receive this event from a component usage. You have to define the
component usage on the properties tab of the view which embeds the above view
in your case. Then you can create an event handler in the view controller of the view
by using F4 and selecting the event from the component usage on the event
column in the methods tab.

Question 67: Assistance class

How can I create an assistance class in Web Dynpro component?

A: When creating a WD component, there is a field called 'Assistance Class'. In here, specify the name you want to give to your assistance class and hit 'enter' and then save. Your assistance class would now be created.

The other way is to create a class from 'se24' that implements the interface: 'IF_WD_COMPONENT_ASSISTANCE' and activate it, and later on assign it to your component.

After the assignment is done, your component controller would have an atttribute called "wd_assist" created which you can use in the future to access the texts.

To add texts to this class, just open the view controller or the component controller and then go to the system menu "GOTO->Text Symbols", here you can add texts and activate your assistance class.

E.g: `wd_assist->get_text( 001 ) will return text with id 001.`

Another way is to create a class implementing the interface:

"IF_WD_COMPONENT_ASSISTANCE". Specify this as 'Assistance class' in your webdynpro component.

In your assistance class, specify all the texts to be used as text elements. A 'get_text' method passing the element i.d. will return you the text.

Question 68: Translated OTR text is not displayed in WD4A application

I have a strange problem with my WD4A application. We developed it in English, created a new Z package for OTR text we are using in the application. Now, I have translated the text into German.

When I open the view in SE80 with log-on language German, then I see the translated text in German. But when I open the application in IE with log-on language German, I see still the Engish text.

What can be the reason for this?

A: This is because the OTR is reading the content from the buffer. Reset the buffer and you will be able to see the updated text in the browser also.

Just execute the transaction "/$OTR" to reset the buffer. You will get a confirmation of the same as a status message.

Question 69: Input Fields in a table

I have created a view which uses the table element. Some columns are defined as 'inputfields'. It is possible to enter several data in different cells.

The questition is how to get the information which rows and columns have been changed by the user.

A: Please check the documentation for "CONTEXT_CHANGE_LOG". There is also a demo component "DEMO_CONTEXT_CHANGES" which demonstrates the use of I in the help section.

You can also check the type of your table column. It must be an 'InputField'.

```
--> Table
--> TableColumn_1
--> TableColumn_1_Cell_Editor --
>Properties(InputField)
--> TableColumn_1_Header -->Properties(Caption)
--> TableColumn_2
--> TableColumn_2_Cell_Editor -->Properies(TextView)
--> TableColumn_2_Header -->Properties(Caption)
--
```

Question 70: Change the visibility property of a WD element

How can I change the visibility attribute of a web dynpro element during runtime?

I implemented a web dynpro which consist 2 input fiels, textview and a button. When the button is pushed, the one on the input field is empty. The visibility of the 'textview' element should be become true.

I tried following:

```
elem_text TYPE REF TO if_wd_context_element.
elem_text = lo_->get_element( ).
CALL METHOD elem_exception->set_attribute_property
EXPORTING
attribute_name = 'EXCEPTION_TEXT'
property = if_wd_context_element=>E_PROPERTY-VISIBLE
VALUE = 'X'
```

But I wasn't successful.

What did I do wrong?

A: It is easier to create an attribute in your context (type wdy_boolean) that represents the visibility of your element. Change that attribute to "abap_false/abap_true" and bind it to the visibility parameter of your element.

Another option is to work with the class methods.
E.g. for 'cl_wd_input_field', you have "set_visible".

```
data: lo_input_field type ref to cl_wd_input_field.

lo_input_field ?= wd_this->m_view->get_element( id
inputfield ).
lo_input_field->set_visible( 01/02 ).
```

01 for not visible
02 for visible

To bind context attribute to visibility property of UI element, it should have type 'WDUI_VISIBILITY', not 'WDY_BOOLEAN'.

'WDY_BOOLEAN' is CHAR(1) and it is not possible to assign 01/02 values to it.

Question 71: Accessing the context

I was looking at the 'WD_COMP_CONTROLLER' attribute. The 'IG_COMPONENTCONTROLLER' interface does not seem to have any explicit attributes for the component controller context.

How can I access the component controller's context from a view method?

A: Map the component controller's context to your view's context by dragging and dropping the particular context node. Then, you can access the context as your view's context itself. When you want the component controller's context shared across multiple views, map the context to each view's context.

The 'wd_comp_controller' attribute is to access methods inside the component controller.

Question 72: Append 10 rows in ALV

On the click of this button, I need to append 10 blank rows to the ALV table.

How can I execute this?

A: Use the 'ONUSERFUNCTION' event handler.

This is where you add the code to append the rows to your ALV table.

Question 73: Hiding a group

I have two groups, GP1 and GP2. GP1 had input fileds and a button, while GP2 has a standard table.

I want to hide GP2 initially and when I clicked on the button, the standard table should be visible.

So in my node which is bound to the table, I am creating an extra node called visible and binding it to the group. On button click, I'm first filling my standard table and then I say "lr_node->set_attribute (exporting name = 'visible' value =abap_true".

All worked fine. The GP2 is hidden. When I click on the button, I get the table. But when I select sm row, then GP2 is not visible. I can't see the table then after selecting a row. I'm missing on something.

How can I achieve this?

A: Check if you are you doing anything on the lead selection.

You are setting the attribute on invisible by default. Only on action you will overwrite the value. In your code, when you go through 'wdmodifyview', the standard values are reset.

You should make an attribute visible, outside your table, e.g. node layout directly under your root context node. I think that you bind now to the selected element of the table, only in the default the attribute is set and not in the lead selection. Bind it at design time to the visible attribute of the group.

You can also check if the "visible" property of the group is bound to the "visible" attribute in your 'lr_node' at design time.

For visibility, you should not use "wdy_boolean (abap_true)" but "WDUI_VISIBILITY" with the following values:

01 none
02 Visible

So your attribute should be of type "wdui_visiblity" and you should set it like this:

```
      lr_node->set_attribute( exporting name =
'visible' value = '02' ).
```

Another example to set it is the following:

```
data:

node_nd_sel_values TYPE REF TO if_wd_context_node,
elem_nd_sel_values TYPE REF TO if_wd_context_element,
stru_nd_sel_values TYPE wd_this-
>element_nd_sel_values ,
item_rel_no LIKE stru_nd_sel_values-rel_no.
* navigate from <CONTEXT> to <ND_SEL_VALUES> via lead
selection
node_nd_sel_values = wd_context->get_child_node( name
= wd_this->wdctx_nd_sel_values ).

* get element via lead selection
elem_nd_sel_values = node_nd_sel_values->get_element(
).

* get single attribute
elem_nd_sel_values->get_attribute(
EXPORTING name = `VIBILITY_FLAG`
IMPORTING value = '02 ' ). /// make it visible
```

This will work just fine even with a 'char01' context attribute set to X or space. The attribute needs to be bound to the visible property of the group in the properties tab. Just check if you have done it.

Question 74: Multiple row selection in the standard table

I have a standard table in my view. I want to select multiple rows from it. I also need to know which rows have been selected.

How can I accomplish these?

How do I read the values of the rows that have been selected?

A: Go to the table properties and give "SelectionMode = Multiple". This will allow you to select multiple rows. The selected rows will be availble in the "WDEVENT" or lead selection.

You can also get all the selected rows of the node using the method "get_selected_elements" of "IF_WD_CONTEXT_NODE" interface.

```
CALL METHOD mo_wd_context->get_selected_elements
EXPORTING
INCLUDING_LEAD_SELECTION = abap_true
RECEIVING
set = lt_elements.
```

Here, "mo_wd_context" is the reference to the context node that you are using for the table.

In addition to the table UI-element property settings, you need to do the following:

In your node properties, set the selection property to '0..n' if your cardinality is '0..n', or else set it to '1..n' if your cardinality is '1..n'.

With regards your second question on how do I get all selected elements of a context node?

You can get all selected rows of the node using the method "get_selected_elements" of "IF_WD_CONTEXT_NODE" interface.

```
CALL METHOD mo_wd_context->get_selected_elements
EXPORTING
INCLUDING_LEAD_SELECTION = abap_true
RECEIVING
set = lt_elements.
```

Next, loop through the above internal table and read the attributes of each element using the method "get_static_attributes( )" of the interface "if_wd_context_element".

Question 75: 'ls_sone' structure

It has the following code:

```
data:
lr_context_node type ref to if_wd_context_node,
lr_context_element type ref to if_wd_context_element.

data:
lt_selected_elements type wdr_context_element_set.

data:
ls_some_structure type some_structure.

lr_context_node = wd_context->get_child_node( name =
'NAME' ).
lt_selected_elements = lr_context_node-
>get_selected_elements( ).

loop at lt_selected_elements into lr_context_element.
lr_context_element->get_static_attributes(
static_attributes = ls_some_structure
).
```

What should be the 'ls_sone' structure?

A: It will be a structure. You can use the web dynpro wizard to generate the code to read the atttributes of the node, and then data declaration would be available for you.

"some_structure" is the structure of your context node. If you have for example a
context node of structure 'kna1', this should be used here.

If you did not assigned a structure to the node, just use "TYPE if_v_viewname=>element_contextnodename" to get the structure of the node.

Question 76: WD ABAP Table 'LinkToAction'

I have added a 'LinkToAction' into a cell of a WD table column. To call the correct action in the event handler, I need to know the selected row and column.

How can I receive this necessary information?

A: In the 'wdevent' parameter of your 'linktoaction', you will have a parameter name 'CONTEXT_ELEMENT' that is of type 'if_WD_CONTEXT_ELEMENT' from which you can get the index of the element in the table. Using this, you will know on which row the action was performed. For a column, you can use the ID parameter means the ID of the ELEMENT, i.e. your link which column link was clicked.

Set a debug point in your action and analyze the event parameter of it. Under that object, see the parameters' list.

Question 77: External Mapping and Component Interface

I wanted to refer to all sub-components via component interface, in order to change the implementation dynamically. But I can not define an external mapping in context of component interface, it is not aktiv. Does it make sense?

The node has only obligatory property "interface node", but not "Input Element (Ext.)".

I have a component A and component interface 'A_IF'. Component usage is defined for 'A_IF'. 'A_IF' is implemented by B, C, and D. During runtime I want to assign B, C or D to the instance of 'A_IF' in the main component A.

The problem is that the context of 'A_IF' can not be set for external mapping.

A: You can't define a comp usage for the interface because you can define it only for the component.

It's not the context of A that needs to be available for mapping, it's contexts of B, C, and D that needs to be available for mapping.

We are using B, C, and D within A. I think this is where you are mistaken.

Question 78: Define mapping during runtime

Is it possible to redefine mapping during runtime in WD ABAP?

A: Yes. You can define a usage of an interface component, and during runtime create any component for that usage that implements the interface component.

For external mapping, you can:

1. Define the interface component with context node (Input Element External).

2. Create a component which defines a usage to the interface component.

3. Go to the component usages folder and open it.

4. Right click on the usage you just created, and choose 'Create controller'
usage.

5. Double click the "interfacecontroller_usage" you just created.

6. Here, you can add a controller usage using the button at the top.

7. Now, you should be able to define the external mapping by dragging the node of the component controller to the "interfacecontroller_usage" node.

Question 79: Bug at Horizontal Gutter UI element

I have a pop-up window with a view on it, displaying some text input fields. The root container has the 'MatrixLayout' set, and I have four columns on my view. Now, I want to separate the input fields from the close button with a 'HorizontalGutter UI' element. In order to display this gutter from one end to the other, I set the 'colSpan' value to "4" because of my four columns. The button has this value set as well to display it in the middle of the view.

Everything works as expected in the layout preview (SE80). I have my input fields in four columns on several lines below the horizontal gutter from one end to the other, and below the button to close the pop-up, centered in the view.

Now, when I activate this view and load the application into the Internet Explorer, and then open the pop-up, I do get my view as expected. The result is the input fields are in their four columns, and the button below is centered at the pop-up window.

The problem is the gutter is only as long as the first column and not as expected which is as long as the pop-up window.

Any ideas why this could happen?

A: You can try setting the Matrix layout width to 100%.

The Matrix layout does not work based on column count. It is only the grid layout that is based on columns. A matrix layout works based on what you specify as the matrix head data and matrix data. So in your case, if you want the gutter to span the whole view, you could specify the width as 100%.

Question 80: Standard table selection

I have a table with selection mode single set, 'readOnly' set, and 'rowSelectable' set. I want to be able to select a single row, which opens a pop-up window (that works fine). The thing is when I load the application and view where this table is displayed, the first row is selected by default. I still can select another row to display the details in a pop-up, but the first row is selected (or highlighted in orange) as default.

Is there any way that no row will be highlighted per default when I load the view/table?

A: In your context node, set initial lead selection to 'false'. It will not come by default as selected.

Another suggestion is to change the selection mode of your table in the table properties as "singleNoLead", and it should work fine. Choose "MultiNoLead" if you want to select multiple rows from the table.

You could also do 'unsetting' the initial lead selection in the context.

Question 81: Table row/cell editable

How can I make one row or a single cell in a table editable?

What property should this attribute is bound?

A: In the context node that you bind to the table, add one more attribute 'read_only' of type char01. Bind this attribute to the 'read_only' attribute of your table field. When you populate your internal table, set the value for this field also as 'X' or space. When you call a 'bind_table' after that, only the rows for which the 'read_only' attribute is null, will be editable. If the attribute is 'X', it will be 'read_only'.

The property is "READ_ONLY". You will see it in the properties tab of the table.

Your table field has to be bound to a cell editor 'input field', and only then this is applicable. For a 'textview' this will not work, because it will always be 'read only'.

The whole table will not be editable. Say you have an internal table with 5 rows, which you will be binding to your context.

If you have a code like the following:
wa-read_only = ' '.
modify itab from wa index 3.

Then, only row # 3 in your table will be read_only.

When you initialize the context, set the 'read_only' attribute as 'X' so that will be default, fields will be 'read only' and not editable.

If you have 5 fields, and all fields with cell editor's input field and bound to the same 'read_only' attribute, then changing the attribute will reflect on all the fields. If you want the behavior at a cell level, bind each column's 'read_only' property to a different 'read_only' attribute. Or if you want some columns always in 'read only' mode, use text views for them and not input fields.

Question 82: Selecting a row in table control

I want to set a row, or a group of row selected based on a particular field value in a table control UI element.

How can I do this?

A: You can use the method "SET_SELECTED" of the interface "IF_WD_CONTEXT_NODE" by specifying the index of the specific rows.

However, keep in mind that multiple rows can be selected only when the "selection" property of the context node is set to multiple, as well the "selection mode" property of the table UI element is set to multiple.

Question 83: Tree Control where leaves are Independent Tables

I am trying to construct a Web Dynpro application for a vehicle ordering scenario. I want to have x number of vehicle families (e.g. represented as a node on a tree) and beneath that node, I want to present the user with a table that has the various vehicle models within that model family. The table rows represent the colours that are applicable for that particular vehicle family.

Here is a crude graphical representation:

vehicle family - aaa (first node of tree)
<MATNR>.................|..<RED>...|..<GREEN>.|..<BLUE>....|..<Total>.|
aaa - auto................
|................|....<N/A>.....|...................|...............|
aaa -
manual.............|................|...................|...................|...............|
aaa -
sports...............|................|...................|...................|...............|
aaa - sports
manual....|................|...................|...................|...............|
aaa - special
edition....|................|...................|...................|...............|

vehicle family - bbb (second node of tree)
<MATNR>.................|<YELLOW>| <PINK> | <GREEN> | <Total> |
bbb -
auto.................|...................|.................|...................|...............|
bbb -
manual.............|...................|.................|...................|...............|
bbb -
sports...............|...................|.................|...................|...............|
bbb - sports
manual....|...................|.................|...................|...............|
bbb - special
edition....|...................|.................|...<N/A>.....|...............|

vehicle family - ccc (third node of tree)
<MATNR>.................|..<RED>......|..<BLACK>.|...<Total>...|

```
ccc - auto.................|..................|.................|................|
ccc - manual.............|..................|.................|................|
ccc - sports.............|..................|.................|................|
ccc - family special.....|..................|.................|................|
ccc - special edition....|..................|...<N/A>.....|................|
```

I do not know how many vehicle families (aaa, bbb, ccc) there are until runtime, as these are dictated by master data. The columns in each table for a given vehicle family have different headings, as of the 27 colours in the palette, certain colours are valid for only certain families, and some colours are only valid for a given vehicle model (MATNR).

Looking at the Hierarchical Table via Key/Parent Key, the column names are the same for all entries in the tree.

I did consider using the Tray UI Container, but I could not see how to put x number on the screen, where x is the number of vehicle families. I could code 20 of them on the screen (one after another) and then make the surplus invisible, but I am after a more elegant solution.

I did try to find the equivalent of a "collapsible area" control that is available in Dynpros, but could not find it.

The tree control would be perfect if I could make the leaf a table, and that table layout independent of the tables for other leafs.

How can I write this UI in web dynpro?

My WD app compiles and all seems good. However, I get a runtime error "ASSERTION_FAILED". The error is raised in 'CL_WD_DYNAMIC_TOOL' in Method 'SET_TREE_LEAD_SELECTION', as the statement asserted 'i_wd_tree' is bound.

I am using the code you refer to above as the basis of my application.

I can't see why it appears. The reading I have done indicates that the object already has values. It can't see where my tree is already populated. Any ideas?

A: It needed dynamic programming with static node. You can use that logic.

Please check out standard example 'WDR_TEST_EVENTS' and in this check for view 'TREE_STATIC_DYNLOAD'. It serves the purpose. Rest data passing and all you can use as per your requirement.

You can put a break point in 'WDDOMODIFYVIEW' method and try to debug the application. Also put break point in create node call so that you can find out where exactly it's going wrong. Check your cardinality of the node and the class also. Hope you will get the exact error.

Implementing the event handlers and controller methods

Question 84: Initialization Context

On a view, I have a context for a table. I need the value 'when visible' for the view properties 'lifetime'.

How can I initialization the context for my table?

A: You could use the method "WDDOINIT" to initialize the context, or you could use a supply function.

If you want to initialize it only once, although the view is removed and recreated, you should map your context node to a node in the component controller or in a custom controller. They will stay, even when the view is not visible.

In the "wddoinit" method of your view, fetch the internal table which you want to bind to your UI table. Then bind it to the context. If this is done in the "doinit", it will be called only once when the view is initialized.

Question 85: filling and locating the node

Does it mean that the data in the table was duplicated each time someone navigates to this view? Does it make the table content larger?

If it does, where is the node located (view or component controller), and how do you fill the node?

When I call the view for the first time, I loaded some data in my Context. The next time I called the view, I want to update the data but I must delete the old data.

Which method or function I will need to do that?

A: To delete the existing binding, use the method "node->invalidate( )". Then, do the binding again for your fresh values. Every time you update the data that was bound, just call "bind_elements" on your node that will update automatically. You do not have to invalidate each time.

Additionally, "bind_table( )" overwrites old elements too.

Question 86: Tree UI Element

I have discovered that the Tree UI Element visual behavior is strange. Is there a way to change this behavior in my coding?

Assuming you have such a tree (fully expanded by the user):

```
A
--B
--C
---D
```

If you unexpanded A and expand again A, then you get (STRANGE_OUTPUT):

```
A
--B
--C
```

instead of (NORMAL_OUTPUT):

```
A
--B
--C
---D
```

In most widget toolkits (for the web or for normal GUIs like), the "NORMAL_OUTPUT" is expected.

A: Check if you have bound the "expanded"-property of the nodes in the first level. You should create a context attribute in the context nodes, which can hold the expanded state. Then you can define the initial state and you can keep the expanded state there, even if the parent node is collapsed.

According to SAP help, default value for "expanded" property is "false". So, if the property is not bound to context attribute, it is going to collapse and state is not stored between user interactions.

Question 87: Exceptions instead of events

I wonder if in the next releases of WD4A, there will be a way to send to an upper level component exception from a component. It would be interesting to have the same behavior as events sent from a component to an upper level component.

Is there a plan to release it?

Is it possible in a components method to define which exception classes can be raised like in a normal method of an ABAP OO Class?

In the methods of a component, I only have the possibility to define the method name and signature but I have not found any way to define the exceptions which can be raised.

How about the usage of dynamic exceptions? From my understanding, it should be possible to throw or catch them without declaring them in advance.

A: If I am not mistaken, you can already pass on exceptions along the call stack of method calls. Since WDA was implemented using ABAP, we have no control over how exceptions are handled and the normal ABAP way happens, which is quite powerful in its own way.

You will not be able to define it in the signature and therefore you can't raise an
exception in view or component controller methods. But if you raise them in a
normal ABAP class, (as model) you can catch it in all calling stages.

In components, you cannot mention the exceptions as an attribute, but you could do it in the code that you write. According to the exceptions, you can invoke events of your choice.
It would be a beautiful functionality if they could implement exceptions at the UI level methods.

Good point about the dynamic exceptions. If you set "CX_NO_CHECK" as parent class of the exception, it should be working.

Exceptions that are defined using subclasses of "CX_NO_CHECK" must not be declared explicitly in the interface of the procedure. The class "CX_NO_CHECK" and its subclasses are implicitly always declared and are always propagated.

Question 88: Passing values to FM through WDP for ABAP

I have an ADOBE form. Once the user enters the details and submits those fields details should be passed to a function module as import parameters to FM. For example, in the ADOBE form I have name and age fields. Once these fields are entered, they should go to a function module as import parameters to it.

What can be the code for this?

I have a submit button. Once the button is clicked, all these values should be extracted from the adobe form and should go to a FM.

In this code, I'm getting the following error in the browser:

Function parameter "NAME" , "AGE" are unknown.

Though I declared Name type "char10", I'm still the same error.

How can I pass these values to an internal table, then to a FM as table? What can be the code for this?

A: To pass the values to the function module, there are two steps:

1. Read the context element attribute (in your case, name and age) and store it into a local variable.
2. Call the FM by using the above variables in the importing parameter.

The code will look like the following:

```
  data lo_nd_node_name type ref to
if_wd_context_node.
  data lo_el_node_name type ref to
if_wd_context_element.
  data ls_node_name type wd_this->element_inputs.

  lo_nd_node_name = wd_context->get_child_node( name
= wd_this->wdctx_node_name ).
  lo_el_node_name = lo_nd_node_name->get_element(  ).
```

```
lo_el_node_name->get_attribute(
    exporting
        name =   `NAME`
    importing
        value = val_name ).

lo_el_node_name->get_attribute(
    exporting
        name =   `AGE`
    importing
        value = val_age ).

call function 'FM_NAME'
    exporting
        name = val_name
        age = val_age.
```

In the above code, replace 'node_name' with your actual node name.

You can also do this if the submit button is within the form.

1. Make the FM an RFC.
2. Wrap it as a "WebService".
3. In the adobe designer-> data view palette, and create a new data connection with the WSDL file created in step 2.
4. Bind the import parameters from the new data connection to the respective fields in the form.
5. Drag and drop the button of this data connection into the form.
6. Test it.

It won't take more than 15 minutes to finish this process.

When finished with the above process, please check the following:

1. Check if you have declared the name and age as the FM's importing parameters?
2. Ensure that you use the same name while calling the FM from Web dynpro.

The following checks should give you some clarity:

In FM definition (se37):
give "ip_name" and "ip_age" as importing parameters.

Then, in web dynpro, declare two variables "l_name" and "l_age"
which are of the same data type as the FM's importing
parameters.

Then, call the method as follows:

```
call function 'SAMPLE_FM'
EXPORTING
ip_name = l_name
ip_age = l_age.
```

Take note that the formal parameters of the FM occurs on the left
side.

Also, ensure that you have activated the function module.

Use of the 'tables' feature in FM is obsolete. Instead, you can put
all your data inside an internal table and pass it as an exporting
parameter. You do not lose any functionality by exporting an
internal table.

Here is how you can create an internal table and insert values to
it:

Create a table and type, e.g. "zuser_details" with the content you
want in SE11.
Choose the 'Data element' radio button and then choose 'table
type'.
Enter a structure name for your table type and double click it.
Enter the structure details - name and age.
Save, activate the structure and then activate the table type.

In your code, you have to create an instance of the created table
type as follows:

```
data itab type zuser_details.
data wa like line of itab.

wa-name = 'name1'.
wa-age = 10.
append wa to itab.
```

```
wa-name = 'name2'.
wa-age = 20.
append wa to itab.

wa-name = 'name2'.
wa-age = 30.
append wa to itab.
```

In the FM definition, specify an importing parameter of type 'zuser_details'. Then, pass "itab" as a parameter to the function module, just like any other parameter.

Question 89: Run time error while running web dynpro

I got the following error while running web dynpro:
My Default view is "INPUT_VIEW".

```
============================================
```
The following error text was processed in the system NSP: The lead selection has not been set. INPUT_VIEW
The error occurred on the application server BomwSAPk210_NSP_oo and in the work process o.
The termination type was: RABAX_STATE
The ABAP call stack was:
Method: _RAISE_ELEMENT_NOT_FOUND of program CL_WDR_CONTEXT_NODE===========CP
Method: PATH_TABLE_GET_ELEMENT2 of program CL_WDR_CONTEXT_NODE===========CP
Method: GET_BOUND_ELEMENT of program CL_WDR_VIEW_ELEMENT_ADAPTER===CP

Is there a way to fix this?

A: The first suggestion is to put a 'tick' mark on the checkbox "Lead selection" in the component controller. Do this for all the context nodes. Then, activate the entire component.

Another analysis is the error appears when an UI element is bound to a context node or attribute on a node, where this node is defined as: cardinality o..n or o..1.

The framework will not create a default empty element in this case. When the view is to be rendered, its source content doesn't exist. As the node has no elements, rendering fails. Now, in your case check for the cardinality. You can try with different cardinalities as per your requirements.

Check also the initialization lead selection property. For cardinality: o..n, selection: o..1, initialization lead selection: false; and for cardinality: 1..n or 1..1, selection: o..1, initialization lead selection: true.

Question 90: Using Enhancement Framework in methods of WD Components

I want to add my custom code to the "WDDOMODIFY" method of a view.

How can I implement the same through Enhancement Framework?

I don't want to add an element, rather in "WDDOMODIFY" method I want to set the default values for some select options already created in a view.

Without 'Post exit' I was able to do, but I want to know how I can go further with 'Post exit'.
So basically, I want to add a source code not elements.

A: You have two options which are PRE EXIT and POST exit. The first one is called before the domodify, and the second one after the domodify.

Question 91: Difference between component controller and custom controller

What is the difference between component controller and custom controller?

What are the types of nodes in a view?

A: For a component, there will be only one component controller, whereas you can have multiple custom controllers so that you could differentiate the controlling methodology used.

There is a normal node and recursion nodes. In the recursion nodes, you can include the same node inside the node, that's why it is recursive. It is basically used in the contextual navigation panel.

There's no Model Nodes like in Web dynpro Java.
There are only Value nodes and Value Attributes in Web dynpro ABAP.

Question 92: Read value of input Field

I have to read the value of the input Field on the click of a button.

For that, I created an application. In the application, I created a start view. In the layout of the
start view, I defined two fields which are input field and button. Then I defined inbound Plug
and the outbound Plug. In the context tab, I created a node 'node1'.

In the node, I defined an attribute of type "String". Then in the layout, bind the input field value with the context node attribute. I also defined the event on the 'onAction' of the Button as "onclick". I also drag the view in the window. Now, my requirement is to get the value of the input field on the click of button in the 'onclick' action.

What is the code that I have to write in the 'onAction' to read the value of input Field?

What type of wizard is used to generate the code?

I used the first option method used in the current controller with my method "ONACTIONON_CLICK".

It generated only the following piece of code:

```
.
method ONACTIONON_CLICK .

  wd_this->onactionon_click(
    wdevent =                          " ref to
cl_wd_custom_event
  ) .

endmethod.
```

A: Create a node in your context and declare an attribute of type string. Bind this attribute to the "value" property of your input field.

Once you enter a value in the input field and click the button, all you have to do is read the attribute value from the context. You can use the wizard to help you with the code.

You can use the code wizard (ctrl + F7) to read the context attribute that you have bound to the input field.

Once you invoke the code wizard using Ctrl + F7, in the dialog window that pops up, just choose the option "Read context/node" and choose your context attribute.

There's also a wizard in your toolbar in the object navigator. You can see it next to the "external breakpoint" icon.

You have selected the option to fire an event. You should select the option "Read context node/attribute" in the wizard.

Then using F4 help, select the context which you want to read. You can directly select an attribute itself. Then the code will be generated. Go through some beginner tutorials which will probably help you with the screenshots.

The option you have chosen is used to call a method. Since you have chosen an event handler method, you have to supply the formal parameters which are not possible.

So, to read the attribute, use the read context/attribute option and select your attribute name.

Before this, you need to create an event handler for your button. This can be done by specifying a name in the 'OnAction' (under 'events') in the properties for the button. Once this is done, just double click on the method name to open the code editor for the event handler.

Once you are inside the event handler, you can use the code wizard to read the value.

Question 93: Change attributes input field

I have a radio button and an input field. I have an action for the radio button. I want to change the method of the action. When the radio button is selected, the inputfield -> enabled = false.

How can I do this?

How can I change the following value?

read_only->defaultvalue = "X"

What is the code for this?

A: Declare a context attribute "read_only" and bind it to the 'read_only' property of your input field. In the event handler of the radio button set this attribute to X or space. It will automatically reflect in your input field.

You can also create one more attribute in the context, type "WDY_BOOLEAN" and give the default value as false which will enable and disable the field on action of the radio button. Bind this new attribute to the enabled field of your UI element, in here is the input field. During the action, set the attribute value = true.

```
To change the value, you can try the following:

Data: mynode type ref to if_wd_context_node.

mynode = wd_Context->get_Child_Node( `MYNODE` ).


CALL METHOD MYNODE->SET_ATTRIBUTE
EXPORTING
* INDEX = USE_LEAD_SELECTION
VALUE = 'X'
NAME = 'READONLY'
.
```

Another way is in the context declare an attribute 'read_only' of type char01.

In the event handler of the radio button,

```
data: lr_element type ref to if_wd_context_element.

lr_element = wd_context->get_element( ).
lr_element->set_attribute(
exporting
name = 'READ_ONLY'
value = abap_true).
```

If you want it to be editable when you launch the view, make the default value of 'read_only' as initial. You can make it true on the radio button event, or vice versa.

You can also do the following:

1.Create a node 'MYNODE' in your view context.

Create three attributes under this node.
a) radio button type xfeld.
b) display type string.
c) enabled type 'wdy_boolean' (make default value as ' ') so that it will not be enabled.

2. Create UI elements.
In your view create the UI elements.
a) Create radio button and bind it with 'radiobtn' from the context.
b) Create input field and bind it to 'dsplay' from the context.
c) Create an action for the radio button on toggle, let it be 'onSelect'.
d) Bind input field enable property to enable from the context.

3. Implement the method 'onSelect'.
In the 'onSelect' method, write the following code:

```
Data: mynode type ref to if_wd_context_node,
myval type xfeld.

mynode = wd_Context->get_Child_Node( `MYNODE` ).


CALL METHOD MYNODE->GET_ATTRIBUTE
EXPORTING
* INDEX = USE_LEAD_SELECTION
VALUE = 'myval
NAME = 'radiobtn'

if myval = 'X'.
```

```
CALL METHOD MYNODE->SET_ATTRIBUTE
EXPORTING
* INDEX = USE_LEAD_SELECTION
VALUE = ' '
NAME = 'enabled'
.
else.
CALL METHOD MYNODE->SET_ATTRIBUTE
EXPORTING
* INDEX = USE_LEAD_SELECTION
VALUE = ' X'
NAME = 'enabled'
.
endif.
```

Question 94: WD ABAP component configurations

We are using WD ABAP component configurations. We understand how to create and change them.

Can we load WD component configurations dynamically at runtime from ABAP, so in case we have scenario 1 we load configuration 1?

A: Yes, you can. First of all you can create different application configurations. You start it from SE80 from the application using the context menu "create/change configuration".
There, you can enter the ids of the component configurations for each component usage. You can create more than one application configuration, which means for each scenario you should create one.

If this does not fit for your application, you can load the component configuration dynamically.

Variant 1: When you instantiate the component, you can pass the configuration key as an optional parameter.

Variant 2: In each component you can load the configuration with a method of the personalization interface. You can do so using the code wizard.

The configuration key is structured as follows:

Create a data of type WDY_CONFIG_KEY

Set the 'CONFIG_ID' to the id you entered in the configuration editor, and keep the rest initial.

Question 95: Reading images from the file system

I want to finish web dynpro for abap program to read some photos from the file system. I may make MIMES in the web dynpro component and create photos in the MIMES, but my boss doesn't agree with me on using it this way. He wants me to read these photos from the file system.

How can I read some images from file system with webdynpro for abap?

Do you think I must use 'fileupload' controller to upload the photos to MIMEs repository?

Are there ways to solve this problem?

A: You can check-out the UI element FileUpload

Question 96: Get the value of a cell if it is an input field in ALV

I have an ALV table with 3 values as material no., description, and quantity.

I need to make the complete ALV editable, and when I entered a value in the material field and press 'enter' the remaining 2 fields should get populated. I have the method to populate the values, but I don't know how to get the value of that cell. I was not able to get it using "ON_CLICK EVENT".

How can I get the value of a cell if it is an input field in ALV?

My requirement is to have a complete editable ALV with all fields as input fields.
When I enter a value under 'material' and press 'enter', I need to capture the
material value. Based on the material value, I need to get the details and populate all those values in the respective fields.

All I need to do is get the material number that was entered. In the pdf of using ALV events, the editable cell editors trigger "ON_DATA_CHANGED" event and non-editable cell editor triggered 'ON_CLICK' event. But I couldn't find the "ON_DATA_CHANGED" event in the ALV events.

How can I find the event?

A: "ON_CLICK_EVENT" you will get a parameter which is "WDEVENT". From that, you will get the current context element, which is the element where you have performed the operation.

The parameter will be "WDEVENT" type "CL_WD_CUSTOM_EVENT", and in the class you will find a method "GET_CONTEXT_ELEMENT" which will return the current row where you clicked (not lead selection). This will give you the input value.

You can also use 'ON Action' event available in each of the column.

You can also try the "on_data_check" action of ALV controls.

To get the event handler to detect the data changes (i.e. the inputs you provide in a particular field), do the following:

1. In the methods tab, create a new method (say 'on_input') and change the method type to 'Event handler'.

2. Place your cursor in the event field and press F4. You will get a popup displaying the possible events.

3. in that popup, choose the line which has 'ON_DATA_CHANGE' or 'ON_DATA_CHECK'. Inside this event handler, you can read the value you have entered and do further processing.

Question 97: Data no longer available after call

I'm not sure what's wrong with my code, but some data is no longer available after I make a call.

A: Make sure to complete the context binding before you make the call. You need to do a binding of your internal table to the context node, and call "set_data" on the alv model. Only then the data will be available.

Question 98: Code errors

I'm still getting the same error at the same place. Below is the latest changes to the code as per your advice:

```
DATA: l_ref_cmp_usage TYPE REF TO
if_wd_component_usage,
l_interface TYPE REF TO IWCI_SALV_WD_TABLE,
* l_model TYPE ref to cl_salv_wd_config_table,
"Contains all characteristics of a table(collumns,
fields, etc)
lt_columns TYPE salv_wd_t_column_ref, " Table type
lt_fields TYPE salv_wd_t_field_ref, " Table type
l_btn_ins TYPE REF TO cl_salv_wd_fe_button,
l_btn_del TYPE REF TO cl_salv_wd_fe_button,
l_btn_sell_all TYPE REF TO cl_salv_wd_fe_button,
l_btn_dell_all TYPE REF TO cl_salv_wd_fe_button,
l_btn_calc TYPE REF TO cl_salv_wd_fe_button,
l_btn_save TYPE REF TO cl_salv_wd_fe_button,
l_function TYPE REF TO cl_salv_wd_function.

l_ref_cmp_usage = wd_this->wd_cpuse_multi_alv( ).
IF l_ref_cmp_usage->has_active_component( ) IS
INITIAL.
l_ref_cmp_usage->create_component( ).
ENDIF.


*Map the interface.
l_interface = wd_this->wd_cpifc_multi_alv( ).

DATA:
node_mdoc TYPE REF TO if_wd_context_node,
elem_mdoc TYPE REF TO if_wd_context_element.
* navigate from <CONTEXT> to <MDOC> via lead
selection
node_mdoc = wd_context->get_child_node( name =
if_create_mass_entry=>wdctx_mdoc ).

l_interface->set_data( r_node_data = node_mdoc ).

*Map the model
wd_this->l_model = l_interface->get_model( ).

*Map the columns
lt_columns = wd_this->l_model-
>if_salv_wd_column_settings~t_columns.

*Map the fields
lt_fields = wd_this->l_model-
>if_salv_wd_field_settings~t_fields.

cl_salv_wd_model_table_util=>if_salv_wd_table_util_st
```

```
dfuncs~set_all(
EXPORTING r_model = wd_this->l_model
allowed = abap_false ). " try abap_true.
```

A: There is only one difference related to the code. I'm highlighting the changes you need to do:

The problem seems to be in the following block:

l_ref_cmp_usage = wd_this->wd_cpuse_multi_alv( ).
IF l_ref_cmp_usage->has_active_component( ) IS INITIAL.
l_ref_cmp_usage->create_component( ).
ENDIF.

*Map the interface.
l_interface = wd_this->wd_cpifc_multi_alv( ).

```
Replace the above code with the following code:
l_ref_cmp_usage = wd_this->wd_cpuse_main_alv( ).
IF l_ref_cmp_usage->has_active_component( ) IS
INITIAL.
l_ref_cmp_usage->create_component( ).
ENDIF.
```

*Map the interface.
```
l_interface = wd_this->wd_cpifc_main_alv( ).
```

If this does not solve your problem, then please check the following:

1. Have you mapped the context node used here from the component controller to this particular view?
2. Have you activated your component controller?

The change is that 'multi' is replaced by 'main'. 'multi' is used only in case of more than one usage of the grid (which I guess is not your case).

One more thing, you need to check if you are populating the context node with values.

Question 99: No CALL METHOD syntax used in Dynpro programming

I found that while writing a code, we didn't use the CALL METHOD.

I.e. TABLE_NODE = WD_CONTEXT->GET_CHILD_NODE('MY_TABLE_NODE').

How can we directly call a method using interface variable e.g. "WD_CONTEXT" without syntax CALL METHOD?

A: The interface will be holding an instance of the implementation class of the 'IF_WD_CONTEXT_NODE' so we can directly call that method without using the call method.

For more clarification, let A be an interface which have three method definitions.

B is a class which implements A (So B will be implementing 3 methods of A, as well as some additional methods of B, let it 2). B will have a total of five method implementation.

So, when I create an instance of B and assign that to a variable of A, only 3 methods will be copied.

You can't directly call from a variable of the interface unless an object is assigned to it.

Question 100: Code Program correction

What can be the correction of this program? I want to understand the concept. This is an example of ABAP OOPs program.

```
REPORT zjt_test_interface.
INCLUDE zjt_test_interfac_class.
DATA : dd TYPE REF TO demo ,
inter TYPE REF TO sample,
inter1 TYPE REF TO sample.
START-OF-SELECTION.

CREATE OBJECT dd .

inter = dd.

call method inter->test. ******No error with this
statement

* inter1 = inter->test. ********** This statement
gives error "Field 'Test' unknown
```

The below code is a separate include program.
```
*&---------------------------------------------------------------------*
*&  Include ZJT_TEST_INTERFAC_CLASS
*&---------------------------------------------------------------------*

INTERFACE sample .

METHODS test .


ENDINTERFACE. "sample

*---------------------------------------------------------------------*
* CLASS demo DEFINITION
*---------------------------------------------------------------------*
*
*---------------------------------------------------------------------*
CLASS demo DEFINITION.
PUBLIC SECTION.

INTERFACES sample .
METHODS : constructor.

ENDCLASS. "demo DEFINITION

*---------------------------------------------------------------------*
* CLASS demo IMPLEMENTATION
*---------------------------------------------------------------------*
*
```

```
*_____*
CLASS demo IMPLEMENTATION.

METHOD constructor.
ENDMETHOD. "constructor

METHOD sample~test.
WRITE : 'Method test of Interface sample executed'.
ENDMETHOD. "sample~test
```

A: I have gone through the program and there is nothing exceptional.

Inter and inter1 are of type SAMPLE (interface) and it has a method test.

In DEMO class, it implements the interface SAMPLE when create object dd (where dd is the type DEMO). Automatically, it will have the method test from the interface SAMPLE and implementation of the method. It depends on the implementation DEMO class.

call method inter->test. ******No error with this statement.

This statement is correct as the inter is type SAMPLE and can hold DD (since it implements SAMPLE). The TEST method will be available there.

* inter1 = inter->test. ********** This statement gives error "Field 'Test' unknown".

But in this scenario, the system expects test as an attribute and the assignment is wrong.

Another analysis is with reference to your code, the line in which you are getting the error.

In general, when we use the assignment operator (=), the data type on either side should be the same or compatible types. In your case, the following things have to be noted:

1. The method 'test' does not return any data. It simply writes some text.
2. The mode of assignment is not correct. As mentioned earlier,

the types on either side of the assignment operation are incompatible.

You can try the following, however, if that is your need. If you want to call the method '
test
' from the interface object '
inter1
', then do it as follows:

```
inter1 = inter.

call method inter1->test.
```

Further, whenever you are calling a method of an interface or a class, it is always better to use the 'CALL METHOD cls_name->meth_name' syntax. Though the 'call method' part is optional, it is considered a good programming convention and the code also looks more professional.

Question 101: Problem while redirecting to URL

I have created Outbound Plug (named exit_plug) in Window of plug type - Exit.

I've also written the code while firing this plug like below:

```
wd_this->fire_exit_plug(
url = 'http://www.sap.com'
).
```

But while running this WDA and firing this code, the system redirected to the url below:

http://www.google.com/?URL=http%3a%2f%2fwww%2egoogle%2ecom

The same url was added as a paramater.

I want to redirect it to simple http://www.google.com only.

How can I achieve this?

A: Use a link to URL element to get this.

Question 102: Not having the same URL as parameter

I have created one WDA that will give the tabular list of output. From this output, I am selecting one entry for which I want to have further processing in another WDA.

So I have to pass several parameters with it, which should be available in subsequent WDA.

That's why I have used the exit plug of window in the first WDA, and passed the data of the selected entry to another WDA. In this second WDA, I analyzed the parameters through the following code:

```
DATA:
wa_url TYPE LINE OF tihttpnvp,
int_url TYPE tihttpnvp.

wdevent->get_data(
EXPORTING
name = if_wd_application=>all_url_parameters
IMPORTING
value = int_url ).
```

By using this code, I am getting my required data as well as the original URL value also.

But I don't want to have the same URL as the parameter.

How can I do this?

A: You cannot directly put the URL like that, it will append only to the existing URL.

```
Follow the code below:

Data:lv_url TYPE string.


CALL METHOD cl_wd_utilities=>construct_wd_url

EXPORTING

application_name = 'Z_MYAPP'
```

```
IMPORTING

out_absolute_url = lv_url.

CONCATENATE lv_url

'?myparam=1&myparam=3'

INTO lv_url.

wd_this->fire_out_plg( url = lv_url ).
```

The problem is with your concatenate statement.You are appending the URL again to your base URL.

CONCATENATE ******str_url **********'?sap-client=' sy-mandt '&sap-language=' sy-langu '&MODE=' item_mode_ind '&MATTER_DEF=' item_pspid
INTO str_url.

Correct it, it will work.

Question 103: What URL to use

In concatenate statement, the first 'str_url' is required as it builds the URL for new WDA, and for additional parameters I only have to use the concatenate statement.

Or do I just simply use http://www.google.com string as URL?

A: I think the problem may be because of the URL parameters.The only problem with the exit plug is where ever the URL wanted to go; it will be appended to the Server URL as a parameter.

The URL which you gave was:

LINK =
http://iwdf1149.wdf.sap.corp:8000/sap/bc/webdynpro/sap/zm atter_all?sap-client=220&sap-language=E&MODE=DISPLAY&MATTER_DEF=C0000148000 000&URL=http%3a%2f%2fiwdf1149%2ewdf%2esap%2ecorp%3 a8000%2fsap%2fbc%2fwebdynpro%2fsap%2fzmatter_all%3fsap -client%3d220%26sap-language%3dE%26MODE%3dDISPLAY%26MATTER_DEF%3d C0000148000000

You can do the following steps.

So let us analyse your URL, the only thing that matters in your URL is the first part.

That is the following:

Part 1.
http://iwdf1149.wdf.sap.corp:8000/sap/bc/webdynpro/sap/zm atter_all?sap-client=220&sap-language=E&MODE=DISPLAY&MATTER_DEF=C0000148000 000

Please check if this part is working alone. If it doesn't, then it's the problem with your code and you need to analyse how you accept the URL parameters.

Part 2.
This is the second part of the URL:

&URL=http%3a%2f%2fiwdf1149%2ewdf%2esap%2ecorp%3a80
00%2fsap%2fbc%2fwebdynpro%2fsap%2fzmatter_all%3fsap-
client%3d220%26sap-
language%3dE%26MODE%3dDISPLAY%26MATTER_DEF%3d
C0000148000000

From the URL, it is obvious that the URL is going as a parameter
to your application. In a normal case, it doesn't create a problem
as your application it will not recognize this part and it will
ignore this. But if it is creating any problem, you can add one
more parameter in your application name URL.

In most cases when we use the portal, we will get the exit URL
through the URL parameters and will be processed further. I
think that's the reason why the system sends the exit URL as a
parameter so that the other application can close it.

Question 104: Portal Eventing: communication between BSP and WD iView

I am doing a portal eventing between WD Abap iView and BSP iView, with the help of the following blog:

I created a page which has both iViews.

But I was not able to trigger the event from BSP to WD.

How can I trigger the event from BSP to WD?

The BSP on the page where the button is not triggering.

What exactly is iView domain?

A: The domain is the first part in your URL, for example www.**xxx**.yyy.com.

In your case, it will be probably the hostname of your computer.

The reason for this is security. The portal eventing was built in Javascript, and in Javascript it is not allowed to access the other frames that are not in the same domain.

Question 105: Webdynpro ALV with input ready fields

I had some years of experience as an ABAP developer. I currently tried a little bit around with WebDynpro for ABAP. I tried to figure out what this stuff can actually do in comparison with the old Dynpro technology.

Maybe it's not the easiest way to get started, but I tried to create an ALV which is enabled for input. At least two particular columns should be ready for input, one with selection help and one for free text (80 characters), so the user can enter some data and save later on.

Is this (ready for input ALV) supported by Webdynpro? I did not find a way to develop some kind of stuff like this. I only managed to display a "normal" ALV without the option to enter data.

A: You can try the following code snipet:

Basically, what you need would be the "class cl_salv_wd_uie_input_field", and the rest could be figured out.

```
Data: lr_input_1 TYPE REF TO
cl_salv_wd_uie_input_field,

CREATE OBJECT lr_input_1 EXPORTING value_fieldname =
'ZZFROM'.
* lr_header->set_text( 'Flight From' ).
lr_header->set_text( 'Fr' ).
lr_column->set_position( 1 ).
lr_column->set_cell_editor( lr_input_1 ).
```

Question 106: Class for IF_WD_CONTEXT_NODE

I have the following questions:

1. Interface "IF_WD_CONTEXT_NODE" is implemented in which class?

2. What do you mean by attribute of an Interface (i.e WD_CONTEXT)?

TABLE_NODE = WD_CONTEXT->GET_CHILD_NODE('MY_TABLE_NODE'). What does it mean?

3. Why do we create objects of Interfaces and not classes that implement them?
E.g. data: TABLE_NODE type ref to IF_WD_CONTEXT_NODE.

4. Can I see the code for the CLASS that implements these INTERFACES?

5. When and where are the objects for the classes created?
(As in ABAP OOPs - CREATE OBJECT <varname>)

How can we call an interface method directly using an interface variable?

E.g: WD_CONTEXT->GET_CHILD_NODE( ) .

Can you send me a simple example code explaining this?

A: The questions are answered accordingly.

1. All implemetation classes in Web Dynpro begin with "CL_WD" prefix, so you can search for the same in se24.

"IF_WD_CONTEXT_NODE" is implemented in the class "CL_WDR_CONTEXT_NODE".

2. 'Wd_context' is a reference to the root node of your context. Thus, whenever you try to read any node in your context, you should start with the root than traverse down the hierarchy.

You could define attributes for an interface, so that it will be available to all the classes implementing the interface.

Here, you are calling a method of 'IF_WD_CONTEXT_NODE' to get a reference to a context node called as ' MY_TABLE_NODE' in your application. Once you get a reference, you can apply various operations on it like reading values or setting values of attributes of the context node.

3. Its not mandatory to always use interfaces, we can use classes as well. However, the web dynpro wizard generates code that uses interfaces.

The purpose of using interface is that you could store the instance of different implementing class according to the situation.

You can not create objects of this class because it is an abstract class (the reason of its none completeness), therefore it has this interface to use it and complete the implementation.

4. Yes you can check the code in the classes. For example, the implementation class for the interface "if_wd_context_node" is "cl_wdr_context_node".

You can go to the 'CL_WDR' classes and see it.

5. The objects are created in different places. For example, if you go to "CL_WDR_CONTEXT_NODE , CREATE" method, you could see the following code:

```
if node_info->_mapping_info-is_mapped is initial.
create object node type cl_wdr_context_node_val
exporting
parent_element = parent_element
node_info = node_info
node_name = node_name
context = context.
else.
create object node type cl_wdr_context_node_map
exporting
parent_element = parent_element
node_info = node_info
node_name = node_name
context = context.
endif.
```

Let the context node be type of "if_wd_context_node", and somewhere in the webdynpro the object will be created which means an object of "CL_WDR_CONTEXT_NODE". During the process, it will be assigned to the interface 'WD_CONTEXT' in the webdynpro. So the interface will be holding an instance of 'CL_WDR_CONTEXT_NODE'. We know that 'CL_WDR_CONTEXT_NODE' implements the interface 'IF_WD_CONTEXT_NODE'.

So when you assign 'CL_WDR_CONTEXT_NODE' instance to 'WD_CONTEXT' (of type IF_WD_CONTEXT_NODE), only those methods which are part of the 'IF_WD_CONTEXT_NODE' will be available in 'WD_CONTEXT'.

You can call this as a kind of type casting. This is how the objects work in ABAP.

For further understanding, let A be an interface which have three method definitions.

B is a class which implements A (so B will have implementation of 3 methods of A, as well as some additional methods of B, let it 2). So B will have a total of five method implementation.

So when you create an instance of B and assign that to a variable of A, only the 3 methods will be copied.

Question 107: Read the current selected row of a table

I have an event handler method called 'ONACTIONSELECT' for the 'onLeadSelect' event of the table UI element. I need the code for this method.

What is the code to read the current selected value of a field from a table UI element?

A: 'CONTEXT_ELEMENT' is the code.

'CONTEXT_ELEMENT' is of type 'IF_WD_CONTEXT_ELEMENT', which directly contains the pointer to the context element in question. This is the context element of the 'dataSource' of a table or multipane, for which the event has been triggered.

If the element is located in a Table, the context element is the element from the row in which the action was triggered (vertical coordinate).

Question 108: 'LogoffURL' for ABAP Web Dynpro

Do we have the 'LogoffURL' for ABAP Web Dynpro?

I would like the WD application to log off to the URL on same browser window.

How can I do this?

I have entered the URL in the SICF. Now, how do I link it to the button, or link to action element to perform the log-off operation?

How do you connect or link the exit plug of the WD Window, to that of link to Action UI Element which is present in the view?

A: You should look in the 'sicf' transaction to the application entry.

Go to the details, in tab error pages-> logoff page, you can enter the URL and do the adjustments.

You could have a log-off or exit button defined on a page, and on clicking that button you could go to a view which does not have any previous page or previous link.

Also, note that the browser back button is not allowed in web dynpro abap so it will not allow you to go to the previous page unless you have explicitly called the view on the press of a button or a link in your application.

Once you fire the 'Exit plug' of your WD Window, this page automatically appears.

The following is the code to get the window reference for plug firing:

```
data: l_ref_ type ref to ig_<windowname>.

l_ref = wd_this->get_<windowname>_ctr( ).

l_ref->fire_<exit plug name>_plg( ).
You can also try the following:
data: lr_controller type ref to
if_wd_view_controller,
lr_window_ctrl type ref to if_wd_window_controller.

lr_controller = wd_this->wd_get_api( ).
lr_window_ctrl = lr_controller-
>GET_EMBEDDING_WINDOW_CTLR( ).
lr_window_ctrl->IF_WD_VIEW_CONTROLLER~FIRE_PLUG(
'plug name' ).
```

Question 109: Refreshing UI Elements

What is the general way to refresh a UI Element when one of its "source" binding has changed?

Is it to rebind the source?

Is there any "hidden" call somewhere that can be performed?

A: After each event (F4, button event) the bindings get refreshed. So when you refresh your binding, you should go by "wdmodifyview". After that, your server event will be changed.

Question 110: call "WDMODIFYVIEW" manually

So do you mean I should call "WDMODIFYVIEW" manually?

A: I mean that when you change the source, you probably read the context into local variable to change it. You should then bind the changed local to the context again, replacing the old values something like:

```
node->get_attribute
change attribute
node->set_attribute
```

Question 111: Modify the content of the table

How can a UI element get refreshed when the data inside the context has changed?

Has the WD4A framework a listener on the M of the MVC?

How can I recall the supply method of my Table UI Element?

I just want to modify the content of the table and I have no precise idea of what is the best way to achieve it.

A: 1. If you just change the value of a context attribute which is bound to any UI-Element, the UI-Element gets refreshed automatically if your change triggers a roundtrip. So, if you change the value inside an action, for example the UI-ELement will be updated.

2. The supply method is only called once, that is in the moment the context node changes by adding a new element. But a supply method is not a must. You can fill the context node with elements or change a certain element in any method (action, inbound plug) you want to by getting a reference to the node and bind a table for example. But as hack, you can call the supply method directly which is not the best design I guess.

I would guess that if you change the binding by calling: lr_uielement->bind_*('NODE.ATTRIBUTE') the change should be visible directly after the roundtrip was triggered.

You should also take note that the UI elements are automatically refreshed if the values of the bound context node changes. So there is no need to do anything.

If you change anything else, you sometimes have to make sure that the context node is updated.

You have different possibilities:

- You change the content of the context node. This makes sense, if you know exactly what must be changed.

- You invalidate the context node. Then the supply function is automatically called again, whenever the node is used. Just call method "invalidate( )" on the context node.

Question 112: more CPU costly

Is it more CPU costly to invalidate and recall the supply method or to change the data of the context node?

A: But to see the changes in roundtrip is needed, isn't it? It is triggered anyway when you change the context in an action handler.

When you have a look at the interface of a supply method, you'll see that it takes the context node to fill and the parent element.

So you just need to get references to the node and element, and you can call the method:

```
supply_something(
node = lr_mynode
parent_element = lr_parent_element
).
```

Please do NOT call supply methods, action handler, or the other hook methods manually. This could lead to unpredictable results. Even if this works today, it may not work in the future and we cannot guarantee that it works.

Question 113: Grouping more than one view in a single window

I want to group three or more views in a single window.

I need an element which is similar to VIEW SET in webdynpro for JAVA.

How can I do it?

A: You can use "ViewContainerUIElement" which you can find under the 'Standard Simple Elements'. After you added as much as you need, you can add the views in the corresponding window. Just right click on the "ViewUiContainerElement" in the window and choose embed view.

Another suggestion is you can use several view container elements (right corner of simple elements). Later you embed the view in the window component to your containers.

In WD ABAP the concept of 'viewset' is not used, instead the "viewContainerUIelement" is used to achieve the same.

Create a main view, say 'v_main', in that add UI control 'viewContainerUiElement'.

Create another view, say v1. Go to the window, and embed this view 'v_main' to the window. You can see then below the view control 'viewContainerUielement'. In that, you can add the view v1 inside this container. So, if you create more containers inside the 'v_main', then you can display more view inside this and the plugs can be created and fired as the same in java.

Question 114: Getting the pressed item value of Tree UI Element

There is a tree like the following:

Tree
Treenode1
tree_item1
tree_item2
Treenode2
tree_item3
tree_item4
tree_item5

How can I get the value of "tree_item1,2,3" after they were pressed?

In this tree, there is one leaf named 'SFLIGHT'. After clicking this leaf, value 'SFLIGHT' will be acquired and will be shown with ALV control.

I just need to get the value 'SFLIGHT', that is the table will be an output of ALV later.

Are there example codes for this?
A: If you want to get the lead selected element, you can use "node->get_lead_selection( )" which returns you the element, and using "get_static_attributes( )" method gets the value of that element.

If you want to get the value when you press some link, have an action handler for that link. In the action handler method, you can get the current element using wdevent's "get_context_element" method (wdevent->GET_CONTEXT_ELEMENT('CONTEXT_ELEMENT') which returns the element. From the element, you can get the values using "get_static_attributes" or "get_attribute" methods.

Define an event handler for the 'OnAction' event of the tree. The method would have 'wdevent' as an importing parameter. You can use the method call "wdevent->get_string('ID')" which will return the UI element ID of the item that has been clicked. Or you can use "wdevent->get_context_element( )".

Refer to the web dynpro component "WDR_TEST_EVENTS" that has various types of trees.

You can also get the value by the following code:

```
data parent_element TYPE REF TO
if_wd_context_element.

parent_element = wdevent->get_context_element(
'CONTEXT_ELEMENT' ).

parent_element->get_attribute( EXPORTING name =
'VALUE' IMPORTING value = tablename ).
```

Then, the table name is 'SFLIGHT".

Question 115: ALV Change of Selected Row ON_CLICK Event Action

Can I change the Selected Row (Lead Select) based on the action click of a value inside the cell of ALV table?

If yes, then how?

A: You can change the lead selection using "set_lead_selection_index(index)" or "set_lead_selection(element)" of 'IF_WD_CONTEXT_NODE' class.

In your view, if you want to change the lead selection in the table, use the node object which is used for displaying the table. You can use the above mentioned methods to set the lead selection manually.

Question 116: Automatically generated Search Help

We determine input help mode as 'Automatic' for an attribute, which has type e.g. "BBP_PROC_ORG" from a structure in the dictionary. If for this type, search help is determined as explicit search help attachment to the data element, when WD Runtime automatically generates a UI element near to an input field to which this attribute is assigned so that search help can be used. But if search help is determined as 'fixed values' from the domain assigned to the field, then WD Runtime doesn't generate such an element.

How can I solve this problem?

A: When the 'dropdown' element is chosen, the list appears automatically. For fixed values, more often this is sufficient. If not, you can go for OVS option.

You can also use "select_options" component.

Question 117: Freely programmed input help

I need to do a freely programmed input help.

I implemented the interface "IWD_VALUE_HELP" in the help component. But I don't know where and how to call the method "SET_VALUE_HELP_LISTENER".

How can I call the method and get the instance of the interface "IF_WD_VALUE_HELP_LISTENER"?

A: This method is called by the framework. You do not have to call it by yourself.

Index